❧ PRAISE FOR ❧
FOODTOPIA

"*Foodtopia* glides gracefully through the increasingly complex world of food. An important contemporary book."
— MARK KURLANSKY, author of *Salt*

"A fascinating account, moving easily across eras, never starry-eyed but always open to the idea that we can do better than we're doing!"
— BILL MCKIBBEN, author of *Deep Economy*

"Margot Anne Kelley has revealed a story essential for our times ... a spirited and beautifully written account of what dreams the soil can hold."
— JANE BROX, author of *Clearing Land*

"Essential reading for anyone wondering not just where their food comes from, but why."
— KATE DALOZ, author of *We Are As Gods*

"This book is a gorgeous cornucopia. Stellar and timely."
— ALISON HAWTHORNE DEMING,
author of *A Woven World*

"These troops of back-to-the-landers have not just held a mirror up to American society, but given us a lodestar so that we might re-find our way, again and again."
— ROWAN JACOBSEN, author of *American Terroir*

ALSO BY MARGOT ANNE KELLEY

Foodtopia:
Communities in Pursuit of Peace, Love & Homegrown Food

Chicory
(with Barbara Bosworth and Elizabeth Billings)

Queen Anne's Lace
(with Barbara Bosworth and Elizabeth Billings)

The Meadow
(with Barbara Bosworth)

A Field Guide to Other People's Trees

The Things About the Wind and other poems

Local Treasures: Geocaching Across America

Gloria Naylor's Early Novels
(Editor)

A GARDENER AT THE
END OF THE WORLD

A GARDENER AT THE END OF THE WORLD

MARGOT ANNE KELLEY

Boston
GODINE

Published in 2024 by GODINE
Boston, Massachusetts

LIBRARY OF CONGRESS CONTROL NUMBER: 2022949991
Library of Congress Cataloging-in-Publication Data
Names: Kelley, Margot Anne, author.
Title: A gardener at the end of the world / Margot Anne Kelley.
Description: Boston : Godine, 2024.
Identifiers: LCCN 2023039462 (print) | LCCN 2023039463 (ebook) | ISBN
    9781567927344 (hardback) | ISBN 9781567927351 (ebook)
Subjects: LCSH: Gardening—Therapeutic use. | COVID-19 Pandemic,
    2020—Influence. | Human ecology. | Autobiographies.
Classification: LCC RM735.7.G37 K45 2024 (print) | LCC RM735.7.G37
    (ebook) | DDC 615.8/515—dc23/eng/20231113
LC record available at https://lccn.loc.gov/2023039462
LC ebook record available at https://lccn.loc.gov/2023039463

First Printing, 2024
Printed in the United States of America

For Kate,
with gratitude and love

I have great faith in a seed. Convince me that you have a
seed there, and I am prepared to expect wonders.
—HENRY DAVID THOREAU

Has it begun to sprout? Will it bloom this year?
—T. S. ELIOT

In seedtime learn, in harvest teach, in winter enjoy.
—WILLIAM BLAKE

❧ CONTENTS ❧

FOREWORD

MUCH AS IT did a century ago, the world broke in two on or about March 2020. The normal of before recedes into memory, a palimpsest eclipsed by what's come since. Days grow indistinct, blur into one another. Untethered from old moorings, time no longer keeps pace with clocks and calendars. Instead, we linger in the long now, the moment stretching tauter, thinner, as promises it will end extend, again and again, beyond a grim horizon.

Only the seasons adhere to the old order; I measure time by the tamarack.

A GARDENER AT THE
END OF THE WORLD

MARCH

I LIVE NEAR THE end of the earth, half a mile from the tip of a thirteen-mile-long peninsula in Maine. This close to the point, terra firma spans less than a quarter of a mile, a sliver separating the Atlantic Ocean to the east from the Georges River to the west.

Much of the peninsula is granite ledge; scattered outcroppings offer intimations of the mass beneath. Tip-ups of spruces felled by storms often reveal they've been standing atop scant inches of soil, their roots stretching horizontally in search of nutrients. As the soil here is both shallow and sandy, we grow vegetables and herbs in raised beds filled with trucked-in loam and homemade compost. The beds are edged with still more granite, the blocks heavy enough to stay put without mortar. Their sun-warmed mass helps heat the soil in spring and delays the hard freeze in fall, adding extra time to our short growing season.

All but one of the vegetable beds sit alongside the driveway, between the road and the house, sited to get the best sun.

Originally, we had eight large rectangular beds, each around six feet by twenty feet. But a few years ago, we reconfigured them so we could add a greenhouse. A brazen cat makes starting seeds in the house fraught; plus, some of the plants we want to grow need more consistent conditions than Maine can provide.

A tamarack is beginning to overshadow the bed closest to the road. The last few autumns, after its needles gleamed gold then dried down to rusty orange, so many landed in that bed that its soil is a little more acidic than the others'. Though we lime it each spring, horsetail has taken root there and is tenacious. Forebears of this ancient weed once grew as tall as trees, as thick as forests; its stunted progeny seem determined to prove their vigor.

Immediately north of the main beds, behind the greenhouse, is a narrow bed oriented perpendicular to the rest. A decade ago, I planted arctic kiwis in a small section abutting the tool shed that, in turn, sits beside the compost bins. A sungrayed cedar pergola stretches over the shed and bins. As the kiwi vines began to climb, we guided them up some trellising, toward the pergola. Each spring, when new vines splay in all directions, we fasten the wildest to others who are better trained. The canopy now stretches three-quarters of the way across the pergola and has become a haven to pollinators and tiny birds. When the kiwi flowers, the air there is filled with their flutter, thrum, and whir. Once flowers give way to fruit, the insects depart in search of purple, but the small birds stay all summer.

Between the garden and the house are five apple trees. We started with twenty-two, me dreaming of an orchard of heirlooms; only those in the lee of the house survived. I think the combination of salty air and foggy days was too much for the whips. On the other side of the house are two small beds. The narrower one contains a single row of scallions, the wider one herbs and medicinal plants; I added a few flowers to it last year because beauty also nourishes.

DURING THE FIRST week of January, I ordered seeds for this year's garden. When they'd all arrived, I put the packages on the dining room table, organized them by type to make sure I hadn't forgotten anything. The leafy greens got stacked together, the beans, the peas, the tomatoes, the flowers. The melons, carrots, beets, and cukes had fewer packets in their piles. Over the years, I've winnowed out some crops completely, like radishes, sweet peppers, and eggplant. On the table, the garden is perfect; each of those packets of potential is just that—gorgeous possibility uncompromised by too much rain or not enough, by flea beetles or weasels or deer, by a gardener with other obligations who falls behind on weeding.

SEVERAL WEEKS AFTER that, on February 11, I had a meeting with the school superintendent for Saint George and a woman from our school board; I've been consulting with them about ways to bring more adult education options to the peninsula, and we were going over my findings. Shasta, the board member, mentioned that her son was obsessed with news about a virulent virus in China.

"He's terrified it'll come here."

"Get him a cool face mask," I suggested. "They're supposed to protect against it."

"He'd never wear one."

"Look," the superintendent interjected, turning his laptop so we could see the screen. He scrolled slowly, showing us face masks adorned with images of animals, military camouflage, superheroes.

"Heck, I'd wear that one," he said, pausing on one with a dragon, the school mascot.

We all laughed.

WHILE WE WERE chuckling in Maine, the director-general of the World Health Organization (WHO), Tedros Adhanom Ghebreyesus, was giving a sobering speech in Geneva, Switzerland, thirty-five hundred miles away. He announced that the official name for the disease caused by the novel coronavirus would be COVID-19. Explaining the rationale for this designation, he said, "Having a name matters to prevent the use of other names that can be inaccurate or stigmatizing." Though nearly all the known cases were still occurring near Wuhan, WHO policy prohibits references to places not only because doing so stigmatizes, but also because viruses inevitably disperse.

A few days later, Ghebreyesus called on social media companies, news organizations, and governments to push back on those spreading misinformation because the glut of fake news was generating an "infodemic." He warned that nations needed to adopt policies that were consistent and science-driven; otherwise, we would be "headed down a dark path that leads nowhere but division and disharmony."

Three weeks after that, the WHO declared the coronavirus a global pandemic. Their scientists believed outbreaks would be driven by something called "superspreading." They worried residents of liberal democracies would be unwilling to comply with necessary containment strategies and that developing countries lacked adequate public health infrastructure to combat it. They hoped to see COVID-19 "spontaneously petering out" but feared that it would "follow a more sinister path such as the 1918 Spanish influenza and take root in populations worldwide."

And yesterday, March 15, after the third confirmed case here in Maine, the governor issued a state of emergency order. All nonessential businesses must close, schools must stop holding classes in-person, and gatherings are limited to no more than fifty people. Already, even mundane aspects of life feel fraught. The supply chains for everything from hand sanitizers to baking flour, paper towels to baby chicks, are stuttering or failing. Instagram is full of pictures of empty grocery store shelves, something I've never before seen in the US.

TO QUIET MY rising anxiety, I've been spending a fair bit of time in the greenhouse watching seeds germinate—which is more interesting than it may sound. Luckily, my midwinter plant lust had been acute; when I ordered seeds, I'd impulsively added two warming mats to an online shopping cart. So, three weeks before I normally start the seeds, and a solid six weeks before I could have planted any in the ground, I start some seed trays. Outdoors, it's 42 degrees, spitty and raw. But in the greenhouse, it's 52, and the surface of the warming mats reaches a comfortable 70 degrees. These mats don't warm the air; they just keep the soil in the seed trays warm. After planting dozens and dozens of beans, cucumbers, nasturtiums, and tomatoes in the seedling trays, giving them water, and settling a clear plastic dome over each tray, I fill a three-gallon grow bag with compost and loam and plant some spinach and arugula in it. With only two mats and limited sunshine, I need to move the trays and bag every few days to give the seeds equal time in the prime warmth and light locations.

In less than a week, arugula seed coats sit, cracked, atop thin, pale stalks half an inch above the soil. As soon as they push the last vestiges of their seed coats aside, the cotyledons unfurl, lobed leaves more clover-shaped than arugula-spiked. They will provide nutrients until the plants grow true leaves. The spinaches come next, their cotyledons long and narrow like slender pairs of grass blades. The seed coats get stuck on the leaf tips, squeezing them together until they have heft enough to spring free. Green beans break through the soil bent over, pale stem napes emerging first. After they right themselves and a pair of thick first leaves emerge, the discarded seed coats grow so translucent I mistake them for water droplets.

Though I've grown vegetables for more than twenty years, I never focused so closely on these details as I do now. The pandemic is transforming the world's usual dimensions, contracting space and expanding time. At high risk for getting sick, I'm afraid to leave home, so planning, planting, and tending to seedlings has taken on extra significance. And with grocery store shelves often empty, knowing we have food stored in seed form is reassuring. I set out to make my pandemic garden thrive.

The warming mats help many of the plants get an early start, but not all of them. Out of a dozen edamame seeds, only one germinated, dying before it was hale enough to pot up. I don't know why the edamame wasn't happy, though I do know seeds sense when the environment is likely to support their well-being and when it probably won't. Until conditions are close to optimal, they remain dormant. Along with warm-ish soil, seeds need water and oxygen. Some impose more conditions, like a set number of hours of daylight or a minimum air temperature; others require fire or need to freeze.

A few species of pine, for instance, have cones coated with dense resin. Only if fire melts the resin can the seeds tumble free. Byblis, a carnivorous plant native to Australia, germinates only after being exposed to smoke from a bush fire. Maine doesn't have fire-loving plants. Here, plants have adapted to endure—and sometimes even rely on—cold winters. Butterfly bush, rudbeckia, lavender, and verbena all have to overwinter in the ground (or be duped into thinking they did) to germinate; cycles of freezing and thawing gradually soften their tough seed coats, making them permeable. Since softening takes more than one freeze-and-thaw cycle, an autumn cold snap doesn't prompt them to germinate, only to be killed when winter arrives.

A hundred and forty million years of evolution have given seeds the tools to wait out uncertain conditions and to recognize when the world is welcoming. I'm taking my cues from them now.

MY INBOX BRIMS with queries from garden-agnostic friends. Do I think they should learn to garden? Is it too late? What should they grow? For folks in New England, mid-March is still plenty early, I tell them, add that they should order seeds right away all the same. Small seed companies are overwhelmed; their pandemic-strained staffs are struggling to fill the unexpected glut of orders. Even large companies are getting swamped. Some are blocking the online shopping feature on their websites for a day or two each week so they can focus on filling existing orders. Seeds for popular items like tomatoes, beans, squashes, and lettuce are mostly sold out. And the overburdened postal system is taking longer than usual to deliver everything.

Of course I want my friends to grow food; I can't think of a better way to manage the stress and uncertainty and general craziness of this moment. At the same time, though, I keep thinking about what happened the last time there was a massive influx of home gardeners. In 2009, during the Great Recession, seven million Americans started gardens for the first time, swelling the ranks of home growers by 20 percent. Hurrying to meet increased demand, Walmart, Kmart, Lowe's, and Home Depot sourced seedlings from industrial breeders in the South. As spring made its way up the Eastern Seaboard, thousands and thousands of seedlings for peppers, tomatoes, squashes, cucumbers, and other popular vegetables were trucked north. Many of the young tomato plants were infected with *Phytophthora infestans*, a water mold that causes late blight on tomato and potato plants. It's the mold that caused the Great Famine in Ireland during the 1840s.

P. infestans is wicked; it spreads spores so effectively they can infect plants forty miles away. And, once established, the blight kills quickly. First a few spots appear on the plant's low leaves; they don't seem ominous, look like those caused by overwatering. But in a day or two, the mold spreads, as do more spores. Soon, the entire plant—along with almost every tomato in the garden or farm field—turns brown and dies. Organic gardeners and farmers have no recourse except to tear out affected plants, burn them or bag them up, and make sure not to plant tomatoes or potatoes in those beds for at least three years.

That August, the chef and good-food advocate Dan Barber published a frustration-laden opinion piece in the *New York Times*, laying much of the blame for the blight on naive home gardeners who bought seedlings from far away. I'm more inclined to blame the suppliers, since they were the ones who sold the infected plants. But I do agree with his larger point: "When you start a garden, no matter how small, you become part of an agricultural network that binds you to other farmers and gardeners," Barber wrote, adding that "late blight spores are a perfect illustration of agriculture's weblike connections. The tomato plant on the window sill, the backyard garden and the industrial tomato farm are, to be a bit reductive about it, one very large farm."

Living near the bottom of a peninsula, growing tomatoes started in Maine, I hoped my garden might be spared. Then my friend Susan, who lives just a few miles north of us, found blight in her garden. A day later, I heard it had infected the small nursery up the street. Inspecting my plants that afternoon, I spied a couple questionable spots, pulled the plants just in case. If it was late blight, maybe finding it right away and sacrificing the infected plants would protect the rest. It didn't; the tomatoes all died.

This year, our roles are reversed: the garden plants are helping me as another plague encroaches.

TENDING SO MANY seedlings helps give my days a shape and logic. Even so, being unable to travel feels grueling. Finding food for body and spirit was much easier when we could visit family and friends, see colleagues in person, go to stores. Now, each errand must be preplanned. My husband, Rob, picks up boxes of preordered groceries curbside, gets medicine at the pharmacy's drive-through window, goes to the post office just once a week. We lean into online retail as never before, stay in touch with folks via Zoom. We're making do, but I rue the lost spontaneous—miss running into friends and acquaintances, spotting something special on sale, speaking to strangers.

In the past, I couldn't always go where I wanted, of course. I've been frightened into abandoning city walks and rural hikes, turned away at the gates of military bases and private communities, hustled back to a tour bus in Cuba, and saved by a taxi driver in Amsterdam. But much more often, I've moved freely. The philosopher Hannah Arendt calls freedom of movement "the oldest and also the most elementary" individual liberty. It's the one taken away when people are punished—when children are grounded or lawbreakers imprisoned. The one border policies and patrols regulate, deciding the fates of those who want to migrate.

What's freeing for humans is fundamental to life. Before life began, movement on earth was compelled, a pure product of physical forces. As asteroids and other planets collided with earth, smashed bits scattered. Volcanoes spewed gases and forced molten rock from deep within to the earth's surface. The moon, formed of aggregating debris, got caught in earth's orbit. In turn, it tugged hard enough to trigger tides. Gravity and electromagnetism determined which whats went where.

Then came life. Long before organisms expressed preferences, simple cells made clear that life itself has wants—persistence chief among them. But if a body stays in one place, its home site eventually runs out of resources. Soil becomes depleted of nutrients, nearby prey are all consumed, refrigerators and cupboards are emptied. So, living beings have evolved mechanisms for dispersing; legs and wings and flagella make moving easy. For sessile species, those who must stay put, evolution has ensured the next generations can leave.

Based on the varied and brilliant array of ways they launch their progeny into the world, I deem angiosperms supreme. Not only that, this huge group—which is comprised of flowering plants with true seeds—has *also* evolved ways to preserve their genes for long periods of time *and* to have long-distance sex, both of which vastly increase their chances of survival. Some angiosperms need only time and sunshine to disperse their seeds. They are plants with double-layered fruit walls, like okra, in which the fibers of the two layers aren't aligned. As the walls dry, tension develops between the layers; when the tension becomes acute, the walls break apart, opening the fruit and flinging the seeds anywhere from a few feet (for okra) to as far as two hundred feet (for the African tree *Tetraberlinia moreliana*). Others—like touch-me-nots and squirting cucumbers—send seeds flying if something as small as a water droplet lands on them when they're ripe. To my lexical delight, such forceful seed ejection is called "ballistochory."

The many, many species of angiosperms who can't go ballistic have also evolved clever dispersal methods, though they must rely on assistance from wind or water or animals. The helicopter wings on maple seeds create mini tornadoes to keep them aloft, and the floss attached to dandelion and milkweed seeds acts like a parachute, carrying the seeds on a breeze. Water lily seeds have a temporary coat with air pockets that keep them afloat; by the time their coatings disintegrate and the seeds sink to the muddy bottom of a pond, they are far enough from home that they won't compete with their parents for resources. Buoyant coconuts, on the other hand, can float hundreds of miles without getting waterlogged. Burring plants get animals to move their seeds by encasing them in barb-covered sacks that stick to hair and fur. Most flowering plants use less aggressive measures; they rely on color, scent, flavor, or nutritiousness to attract an animal's attention, often benefitting their benefactors.

Winterberries, for instance, redden up in autumn when so many other plants are fading. Midwinter, the bright berries stand out against the snow, easy for hungry birds to spot. But winterberry plants aren't feeding the birds out of kindness; they're using the birds to disperse their seeds farther afield than wind could carry them. Similarly, humans ferry seeds because we like the flavors, rely on the caffeine, value the oil, or appreciate the buzz they supply.

I'VE BEEN FASCINATED by seeds for almost as long as I've been growing food, an interest that extends to seed-saving and seed-sharing. Seeds weave themselves into human cultures, make their presence felt. How we value them tells us as much (or more) about ourselves as about the seeds. Seed-saving organizations work to keep unusual cultivars available, and I buy most of my garden seeds from them. I've also had the chance to visit a few actual seeds banks, including a regional collection here in Maine and one focused on arid-climate plants in New Mexico. Though the seeds those two banks preserve differ, both are charmingly old-fashioned, their haphazard collection of refrigerators and freezers filled with carefully labeled jars, many of which once held jams and jellies.

The seed bank that obsesses me, the ultima Thule of seed-saving, is the Global Seed Vault on Svalbard, a Norwegian archipelago between Norway proper and the North Pole. Built into the permafrost, the vault is basically a series of tunnels and very cold, austere rooms. Necessarily quixotic, it houses the germ lines of more than a million plants in a place so inhospitable none of them could grow there. As incredible as the Global Seed Vault is, as much as I yearn to visit it, Svalbard also feels like the apotheosis of millennia of questionable, often bad, decisions about how we humans treat the rest of the natural world, including the parts that directly nourish us.

Nicknamed the "Doomsday Vault," Svalbard opened in 2008 as a stronghold to protect the crop seeds humans will need if we face an apocalypse. While the only withdrawal so far was triggered by civil war in Syria, the direst apocalypse we'll face is likely to be agricultural, the gradually unfolding crisis caused by climate changes. Incredibly, just thirty crops account for roughly 95 percent of our diets, and even modest changes in growing conditions can lead to crop failures. As that happens more frequently, we'll need the array of genetic material stored at Svalbard to breed new seeds that can thrive in altered and less stable environments.

In 2017, unusually warm conditions in the far north led to so much ice melting that water flooded into the vault. The water didn't breach the rooms where the seeds are stored, but the fact of the flood is a reminder that the forces against which the Vault is meant to safeguard may be inexorable, that our efforts to guarantee a future food supply—while massive—may not be enough.

I KEEP ADDING seed trays to the counter in the greenhouse; the new ones contain melons, squashes, marigolds, cucumbers, and four-o'clock seeds. I also start a container of a shelling pea called Sutton's Harbinger; its vines are short enough that it can grow in a large pot. The trays now stretch across three-quarters of the counter, well beyond the corner with the warming mats, so I brought out a space heater to keep the air above freezing at night. I'm not sure whether it'll work, but it's worth a try.

Getting the garden off to a strong start seems especially urgent this year. Though it's still just trays of seeds and seedlings, I've taken to calling it "my pandemic garden." Already, it feels like more than a way to stay in the moment while cultivating food. I think of it as defiance incarnate, a way to propagate life and health and pleasure and optimism when death feels terrifyingly present.

I WANT TO think of seeds and viruses as each other's opposites—the former beneficent, rewarding those with whom they coevolve, the latter selfish, killing those on whom they rely. Such a simple dichotomy would be emotionally reassuring. The problem is that it's false.

Recently, I started researching pandemics and viruses to better understand what the novel coronavirus may portend. A friend thinks I'm bonkers to be reading books about the Spanish flu right now, but knowing what happened then makes me feel like I can extrapolate, can imagine ways forward for me and Rob, for our families and community. I told my friend that the historian David McCullough said that "history is a guide to navigation in perilous times," an observation that did not appear to alter her assessment of my reading choices. But I think McCullough is right: even though they're imperfect guides, historic pandemics may be our best source for understanding what's coming. Especially because newspapers aren't cutting it. The facts they provide about the coronavirus and the current pandemic are incomplete, changing almost daily, and often colored by biases. I need to know more to put the information they do include into a fuller context.

ODDLY ENOUGH, I'VE learned that viruses and seeds have a lot in common. Like seed-bearing plants, viruses have two discrete life stages—one of prolific growth and reproductive activity and one of stasis. When viruses are in a host, they are active, using the host's cells to make millions of copies of themselves. But when they aren't—when they are resting on a doorknob or sitting atop a package of noodles someone touched at the grocery store or anywhere else outside a living host—they are largely inert. They still have all their genetic material, will rev back into action when they find an appropriate host. But until that happens, they are like unplanted seeds, dormant until conditions are ripe for reawakening.

THROUGH A QUIRK of history, seeds and viruses are also linguistic kin, though the word "seed" has barely changed in centuries. In Old English, the word was *sed, sæd*, meaning "that which may be sown; an individual grain of seed; offspring, posterity." *Sed* came from the Proto-Germanic *sediz* or "seed," which was also the source for similar sounding words in Old Norse (*sað*), Old Saxon (*sad*), Old Frisian (*sed*), Middle Dutch (*saet*), and Old High German (*sat*). Seed, I cannot resist saying, did not fall far from the Indo-European Language Tree.

But its Latin counterpart, *germen*, has undergone a sea change. Originally meaning seed or sprout, *germen* gave rise to the English word "germ," which meant "that portion of an organic being capable of development into the likeness of that from which it sprang: a rudiment of a new organism," a sense that can be traced back to 1644. "Germinate" and "germ cell" are among the few words that still retain the original connotation. In the second half of the 1800s, Louis Pasteur, Joseph

Lister, and Robert Koch, among others, proposed a new theory of disease origin: they believed microorganisms could invade a body and make the host ill. This notion is now known as "germ theory." Since that name was coined, the word "germ" more often means a microorganism, particularly one that causes disease, than it does a rudimentary new organism.

BOTH SEEDS AND viruses also share dispersal strategies, including their penchants for hitching rides from people. Even before *Homo sapiens* arrived on the scene, our predecessors were wanderers. *Homo erectus*, the hominids who learned to use fire at least eight hundred thousand years ago, weren't content just sitting around, staring into the flames. Instead, as climate change caused the forests in Africa to decline, *H. erectus* moved to the savannah and then traveled widely in search of food. As they made nutritional gains, their brains grew larger and more complex. By the end of the Pleistocene era, our direct ancestors, the early *H. sapiens,* had emerged as one of *H. erectus*'s evolutionary progeny, migrated out of Africa, and settled on six continents.

During those long-ago travels, our ancient ancestors discovered new seeds, plants, and creatures they could safely eat, and they carried some of those discoveries to new locales when they migrated, be it seasonally or permanently. Likewise, they encountered novel pathogens and ferried some from place to place. Everywhere they went, they altered the ecology; like Heraclitus's river, not a single place our forebears stepped remained the same.

Those early *H. sapiens* were hunter-gatherers. In his book *The Triumph of Seeds*, conservation biologist Thor Hanson describes the transition from hunter-gatherer to agriculturalist that occurred at Tell Abū Hureyra, an ancient settlement near modern-day Aleppo. Remains there reveal that the sedentary hunter-gatherers living there "enjoyed a diet of more than 250 different wild plants, with 120 kinds of seeds, including at least 34 different grasses" as well as fish and animal meat, notably gazelle.

But around 12,900 years ago, a dramatic temperature shift led to a prolonged cold period, the Younger Dryas, during which finding enough food nearby was nearly impossible. Almost all the inhabitants of Abū Hureyra left, and archaeologists conjecture hunger prompted them to transition from hunting and gathering food to farming it. They gradually figured out how to domesticate cereal grasses and turned them into staple crops. When climate conditions improved and Abū Hureyra was resettled, its inhabitants were farmers, not foragers.

Domesticating cereals was time-consuming and far from simple. At the top of a shaft of a cereal grass is a spike of overlapping rows of seeds and thin quills called awns; each row of seeds and awns is a "spikelet." In wild wheats and barleys and other grasses, spikelets scatter readily once the seeds are ripe. That strategy—called shattering—worked well for the plants; the seeds didn't fall off prematurely and didn't require much outside assistance to disperse. But it wasn't good for humans who wanted to harvest the seed: threshing knocked the ripe seeds off, scattering them on the ground, and left unripe seed on the stalk. Fortunately for our forebears, only a couple genes control shattering, and mutations in them caused some plants to not shatter. Without outside intervention, the population with this mutation would have stayed small. But what was bad for the plants was good for the humans.

Whereas the ripe seeds of shattering grasses were dispersed by the force of a sickle blow, the ripe seeds on the nonshattering plants weren't. So, harvests ended up including ripe seeds from the nonshattering grain plants, along with a medley of unripe seeds from both kinds. As a result, even without knowing to or trying to, early gatherers collected more seeds from the nonshattering plants than the others. Each year, the proportion of ripe seeds planted and harvested from nonshattering plants gradually increased. According to the biologist Jonathan Silvertown, within three hundred years, all the plants those early farmers grew would have been nonshattering versions. But becoming agriculturalists also significantly narrowed their diets. Instead of eating many different foods, the new residents of Abū Hureyra relied on just a handful; Hanson noted that the "panoply had shrunk to lentils, chickpeas, and a few varieties of wheat, barley, and rye." Similarly, in China, our Neolithic ancestors turned rice and millet into staples; those in Africa relied on sorghum and those in South America on maize and beans.

MOST OF THE time, domestication is described in terms of humans making a wild plant more useful (or turning a wild animal into a tamed companion). But just as importantly, domestication is a process of making ourselves essential to another species' survival. Early agriculturalists grew plants that needed them, that were dependent upon them. Without human help, the mutant populations would have plummeted.

Those mutant grasses relied on our forebears just as much as the humans relied on the mutant grasses. They became co-dependent. When the Younger Dryas cooling period ended and climate conditions improved, the trend toward agriculture and away from nomadic hunter-gatherer culture continued, even though an early agriculturalist's life was far harder than a hunter-gatherer's. Early farmers had poorer nutrition than their predecessors, were shorter in stature, had briefer lifespans. Skeletal remains from Abū Hureyra reveal collapsed vertebrae and other deformities caused by the arduous, repetitive work involved in manually grinding grains. Even though a cereal-based diet took a serious toll on human well-being, the early agriculturalists persisted on a path to near-total dependence on a handful of plants. People carried domesticated grasses wherever they went and abandoned hundreds of other plants and seeds on which they had once relied.

LIKE OUR ANCESTORS, contemporary humans eat a lot of cereal grain. But most home gardeners don't grow cereals. They take up a lot of space and lack the visceral appeal of, say, an heirloom tomato. This year, the only cereal I'm growing is flint corn, an especially beautiful version with a rainbow of kernel colors.

Twice, I tried to grow wheat, with little to show for it. A decade ago, a company from whom I often order seeds started offering two-pound bags of Black Winter Emmer. Having never seen anyone plant wheat in real life, I resorted to mimicking

Jean-François Millet's *The Sower*, throwing the grain in wide arcs to fill a one-hundred-square-foot garden bed. The resulting patch was wildly uneven. But it turns out that two pounds was ten times as much as I should have used; by July we had a tall stand of pertly green grass, and by August anthem-worthy amber waves of grain.

All summer I gushed about how easy wheat growing was: it didn't need any help getting pollinated. The wind handled that. All it required from me was watering if we had a streak of dry days and weeding the vetch that seemed determined to coil around the stalks. Then came time to harvest. After cutting the stalks with trimming shears, we laid them on old bedsheets to finish drying, then trimmed the heads—one by one. These we put into a faded pillowcase, which we smacked against the garage wall to separate wheat from chaff. But I'd made the mistake of planting winter wheat in the spring; the entire bed of wheat yielded just a few handfuls of berries, not enough to mill.

Fast-forward five years. From the first foray, I knew to plant spring wheat in evenly spaced rows; that time I chose Red Fife. According to legend, a man dropped his hat into a load of Ukrainian red wheat on a ship moored in Glasgow harbor. When he recovered the hat, he spotted a few seeds stuck to the headband and sent them to a farmer friend in Canada. In 1842, that friend, David Fife, grew the seeds and found they did quite well in that climate. Soon, Red Fife became so popular throughout Canada and the United States that it was the default wheat for decades. A fantastically malleable grain, Red Fife has enough genetic variability to thrive in many different growing conditions; plus, it can be hard or soft, grown as winter or spring wheat. And it tastes great; one grain company describes bread made with it as having "profoundly herbaceous and nutty fresh wheat flavors, a moist, satisfying crumb, and a lovely crust with deep, toasty caramel notes."

Despite being delicious and versatile, Red Fife nearly went extinct. It all but disappeared in the early twentieth century, displaced by Marquis, a cross between Red Fife and a wheat that ripened more quickly. In 1988, beginning with just a single pound of wheat, a small group of Canadian growers worked to bring Red Fife back from the brink of extinction. Red Fife fared better in my garden than Black Emmer did; still, once milled, the flour was enough for just four loaves. But oh, those loaves! Made from grain I'd grown and sourdough starter that Rob wild-fermented, they were our homeplace—its air and water and soil—in the shape of a boule.

THOUGH I LEAVE the wheat growing to others now, I include a lot of unusual plant varieties in our garden. I want to help keep these underappreciated plants alive, for their sakes and for ours. As one person, I can't do much to stave off the mass extinctions the world is facing right now, the unbelievable loss of biodiversity affecting everything from insects to large mammals. But I can grow historical plants, can keep their germ lines alive. My garden is a living library, a compendium of endangered and storied plants interspersed with contemporary favorites. The old, unusual plants have the added benefit of often being quite tasty.

Even old cultivars known for their terrific flavor are hard to find in markets, usually because they need to be picked by hand, or don't transport well, or have short shelf lives. Sometimes, it's simply that they aren't pretty. One of the cucumbers I grow, Sikkim, is shaped like a well-worn nerf football and has a reddish-brown, scaly surface reminiscent of alligator skin. I have never seen it in a store or a farmers market, which is a shame, as its inelegant exterior belies an inner beauty: Sikkim remain firm after being picked for far longer than most commercial cucumbers, and they have a complex, delicious flavor.

FOODS BEING ABANDONED because they are too labor intensive or too delicate or too niche is nothing new. The number and variety of food plants humans rely on began dwindling as soon as those early agriculturalists learned to farm. For millennia, though, the losses were obscured by the limitations imposed by poverty, on the one hand, and by the discovery of novel or exotic plants the wealthy could enjoy, on the other. Plant hunters would travel widely in search of new species, bringing them home to be used as food or medicine or for religious rituals. Almost all the best-known plant hunters have been men, but the first famous one was a woman, Queen Hatshepsut, the pharaoh of Egypt from 1479 to 1458 BCE.

Hatshepsut was the daughter of a pharaoh, Thutmose I, who reigned from approximately 1506 to 1493 BCE. When Hatshepsut was around nine or ten, her father appointed her God's Wife of Amen, one of the most powerful roles a woman could have then in Egypt, and one usually accorded to the wife or mother of the pharaoh. As the God's Wife, Hatshepsut acted as an emissary between Amen and her father;

through that role, she learned to navigate religious, economic, and political demands.

When Hatshepsut was a teen, her frail, young half brother became the next pharaoh, Thutmose II. He married Hatshepsut, almost certainly to firm up his right to the throne. As Thutmose II was underage when he came to power, Hatshepsut's mother stepped in as his regent. Together, she and Hatshepsut wielded authority as they guided the child king. Like his own father, Thutmose II had a son with one of his minor wives who succeeded him as pharaoh when Thutmose II died. Thutmose III was two years old at the time, so Hatshepsut became his regent. However, instead of resigning herself to that role, Hatshepsut declared *herself* pharaoh. In making this audacious power grab, she claimed a twofold genetic right to rule, one based on being her father's child and one, much more importantly, based on being sired by the god Amen-Ra. During a public festival, with many there to witness it, Hatshepsut said she'd had a revelation from Amen-Ra, who told her he was her true father and she was destined to rule all of Egypt.

Twenty-first century American that I am, I can't help wondering if Hatshepsut believed her own hype. Maybe she did. It certainly served her well: as one Egyptologist put it, "her political authority over Egypt stemmed specifically from this sacred position—not as wife of the king, not as mother of the king, not as sister of the king, but rather as wife and daughter to a god."

Like all pharaohs, Hatshepsut had a vested interest in the agricultural well-being of Egypt, for her reputation was tied to it. If the gods were pleased, they flooded the Nile, topping the lowlands with a nutrient-rich layer of muck in which to grow essential crops. If they were not pleased, they would withhold the rains. But Hatshepsut's agricultural interests went beyond the ordinary. She organized a flotilla to embark on a multiyear trip to Punt. As had several previous pharaohs, she ordered the fleet to acquire myrrh, frankincense, gold, and antimony. But she was the first to order a fleet to also bring back live trees. Their successful trip cemented her reputation as both a great pharaoh and a plant hunter. A relief in Hatshepsut's temple celebrating the expedition includes a depiction of men loading trees as large as themselves onto the ship, their root balls cradled in baskets to keep them safe. Text accompanying another image, one of trees standing in containers, describes them as "the wonders of Punt." Those wonders were *Boswellia sacra* and *Commiphora*, the trees from which frankincense and myrrh are derived. Both incenses were critical to many Egyptian rituals, so being able to grow the trees (rather than paying traders for the resins) would have been a huge coup on top of her success in spearheading the Punt fleet.

But future pharaohs also sent traders to Punt for incense, suggesting the trees didn't thrive in their new environment. One Egyptologist proposed the crafty Puntites didn't tell the Egyptians how to nurture the plants or deliberately gave them misinformation to sabotage their cultivation efforts so they could retain the Egyptians as trading partners. Of course, it's also possible the Egyptians were just too aggressive in trying to get resin from the trees. Exotic though they are, myrrh and frankincense have an unglamorous origin: they are basically gooey tree scabs. To get an incense tree to generate resin requires cutting it deeply enough to wound it, but not so deeply that it's seriously damaged, a process called "gummosis."

Despite the many references to Punt left by ancient Egyptians on papyrus and stone, and despite the ardent efforts of scholars since, no one now knows the precise location of the ancient land of Punt.

MY OWN RITUALS don't incorporate myrrh or frankincense or anything more exotic than coffee beans, though I'm starting to think I'd be more content if I had more incense and less caffeine in my life. I begin each day consuming too much coffee and bleak news. The latter now includes checking a website that tracks COVID-19 infections and deaths. Every day, the numbers tick up. The hundred thousandth COVID-19 case was documented on March 6, about three months after the first known case. The two hundred thousandth occurred just twelve days later, the four hundred thousandth five days after that, and the eight hundred thousandth today, March 31. The doubling time is getting shorter, even as the number of cases it takes to reach it grows. We're going in exactly the wrong direction.

APRIL

꩜ ꩜

THREADY WISPS OF the lichen *Usnea* festoon the branches of the surviving apple trees. They're easy to see at this time of year, as the branches are otherwise bare. Like all lichen, *Usnea* isn't really a single being; it's a symbiotic collaboration between a fungus and an alga. The alga photosynthesizes energy, while the fungus's strong cell walls surround and protect the delicate powerhouse. Some of the *Usnea* clumps are new this season, but most have been growing for years, becoming longer and thicker with time. Though *Usnea* looks flimsy and pallid, it is remarkably durable: if undisturbed, it can live for decades, even centuries.

INITIALLY, DOCTORS THOUGHT elevated temperatures were a strong indicator of COVID-19. But now, they think a low blood-oxygen level is a more reliable sign. That's why our friend Tom, a clinician who's the CEO for the helicopter ambulance service here in Maine, stopped by this morning to give us a pulse oximeter. The tiny device has a small plastic clip that fits over a fingertip; it uses light beams to measure how much oxygen is in the blood. We put it on the hall table, alongside the oral thermometer, face masks, homemade hand sanitizer, bleach solution, and cleaning cloths we keep there now.

TOM IS PART of our "bubble," six of us who hope to be able to spend time together in person. But with worldwide cases topping a million, and more than fifty-thousand people dead, we're sticking to Zoom visits for now.

The CDC isn't recommending that people form bubbles; to the contrary, they're urging people to associate only with others in their household. But our friend Kate, who's a public health professional, proposed the bubble. She feels sure the pandemic will last a long time and that we'll need a way to safely gather with folks beyond our closest kin. Being asked to join the bubble got me thinking about kids picking teams in grade school, about the politics of high school lunch tables, about the many, many ways in which we humans organize ourselves into collectives. Scientists suspect that developing the ability to become collectives is one of the reasons our species survived while Neanderthals and other hominids did not.

Learning to live and work together well required that early *H. sapiens* domesticate *themselves*. As with domesticating other animals, self-domestication involved selecting for traits that make *H. sapiens* safer and more pleasant to be around, traits like friendliness, cooperativeness, and reduced aggressiveness.

Women played an important role, of course, by choosing sexual partners with the preferred qualities. The anthropologist Richard Wrangham believes selection also happened at the community level, that groups or tribes killed violent bullies and others who threatened their collective well-being.

Cultivating cooperativeness and friendliness helped early humans collaborate, which enhanced their sense of being part of a coherent social group. But the flip side to prizing group identity is developing an us-versus-them mentality, in which those who aren't part of the group are regarded as enemies.

As somewhat of an introvert—and a person who lives in rural Maine—I thought I would be okay with socializing less. During bad winter storms, Rob and I often go several days without seeing anyone else. But hunkering down to wait out storms did not, it turns out, prepare me for the solitude of pandemic lockdown. I think that's largely because I know storm solitude is very temporary; we usually get plowed out within a day or two, regain power and phone service soon after. Pandemic solitude is harder to bear, not only because we don't know how long it'll last, but also because we aren't physically cutoff. We must concertedly avoid social contact, even with people we love—which feels unnatural because it *is* unnatural.

When lockdown began, I organized a COVID-19 task force for our town because the selectboard and town leaders weren't doing anything to address the crisis. I'm not an elected official, but I know how dangerous a lack of knowledge can be, how quickly nonsense and gossip and rumors will fill a void. If we don't have whatever information is available, and don't have a way to vet what we hear, we can't make good decisions, can't look out for one another.

So, a dozen of us participate in a weekly Zoom call to share information and supplies. The community librarian shares the latest in the ever-shifting recommendations for how to clean various surfaces, the school superintendent the most recent guidelines from the Department of Education. The woman who runs the food pantry tells us what new hurdles the supply chain disruptions are causing. The president of the Small Business Alliance tells us what his constituents are most worried about. Members of church communities tell us what they can do to help, what their congregants need. The head of the ambulance squad shares as much as she feels able to within HIPAA limits. We are beyond lucky that Kate, the public health expert, offered to be on the task force. She stresses the basic strategies for limiting risk, corrects misinformation, tempers unrealistic optimism.

Kate and I also join members of other community task forces from around the state on a weekly Zoom and yet another call with a handful of public health officials. The conversations on these calls are blunter, more tactical, than on our local calls. Everyone participating in them knows the pandemic won't be over by Easter, President Trump's promises notwithstanding. And we realize calling it a "marathon" isn't apt, despite many pundits saying so. No, this is going to be more like an extreme triathlon, one for which almost no one has trained. Each phase will be difficult in different ways, all of them exacting painful tolls.

AFTER THE CALLS, I tend my seed trays, search for hints of green against the mix of loam and perlite and peat moss. A squash germinates on April 2. The first wisp of poppies appears on April 3. A snap pea and a filet bean on April 6. By far the smallest are the poppies, threads so fine I fear even a dribble of water is a pummeling they can't withstand. Yet within days, they push away the last vestiges of their seedcases, stretch strong and wide, stake out their space.

On good days, those signs of life are almost enough.

EVEN WITHOUT THOSE green tendrils, I would know spring is slowly approaching. Well before dawn each day, I lie in bed listening to atonal music—compositions of clicks and pocks, pings and straining squeals, pops and snaps and tic-tic-tic-tic-ticking I imagine John Cage would have loved. The instruments responsible for the night music are assorted parts of the house, woods mostly, in concert with stone and glass and metal, unevenly expanding as the warmer, moister air of spring slowly returns. After being buttoned up for months, the house is awakening from its winter dormancy.

What, I wonder, would seeds breaking dormancy sound like if I could tune into their faint register? What is the music of moisture softening a seed coat, of germ expanding, growing so plump the coat eventually cracks? What racket do the first rootlets make when pushing soil aside? Do the first leaves breaking through the earth's surface and stretching toward the sun sound joyful?

AROUND HERE, THE noisiest, most emphatic intimations of the world reawakening come from spring peepers. Having hibernated all winter, they rouse in April. Peepers live in woodlands with streams and ponds and swamps. Our house is too close to the ocean for the peepers' taste, but our old house was nearer the middle of the peninsula; with a broad swale in the backyard and forty acres of woods next door, it was peeper replete. On spring nights, when the males sang their whistle-y courtship song, I'd sit on the back porch listening, almost as enamored as a lady frog. While I know peeper song is, technically, a plea for sex, to me it's an ode to renewal, a celebration of spring's arrival.

Though male peepers far outnumber females, the males work together to attract mates, singing as a huge chorus comprised of many trios. In each trio, the oldest, largest frog goes first; the frogs repeat their musical rounds all evening, always in the same order. The younger frogs are mostly filling out the chorus; lady frogs prefer the older, larger, deeper-voiced males. Though a single note sounds shrill, when that one note is produced again and again by hundreds of frogs in concert, peeper song seems euphoric, even giddy.

As soon as a frog is chosen by a female, he abandons his chorus-mates. The male climbs onto the female's back for the act itself; afterward, he stays there until the female reaches the watery spot where she'll deposit the fertilized eggs. The male stays atop her not out of solidarity, but to make sure she doesn't mate with another frog on her way to the water. If he planned on being a high-involvement parent, this desire for paternity assurance would make sense to me. But once the eggs are deposited, the frogs go their separate ways and leave their young to raise themselves.

My first pandemic excursion is to find a big chorus. After promising Rob I won't get out of the car, after donning a KN95 mask and medical-grade nitrile gloves, I go into the garage for the first time in five weeks. I have to sit in the parked car for a few minutes and get reacquainted before heading north. Five miles up the peninsula, where Ripley Creek leaves the marsh, I pull onto a broad, sandy berm. As soon as I turn the car's engine off, even before opening the windows, I can hear the peepers: the air fairly roils with lusty song.

TO MOVE AND to be moved. Life can, *must*, move. But to be moved, to be lifted out of the self for a moment, to be briefly assured of something more, is—I think—the glorious recompense we get for being human.

MOST OF THE seeds in the seedling trays are germinating; many have their first true leaves. When I added the second round of trays, I planted two dozen melon seeds, six each for Charentais, Petit Gris de Rennes, Noir des Carmes, and Melone Retato Degli Ortolani. On April 8, the first of the Petit Gris de

Rennes germinated, with the first Noir des Carmes arriving on the ninth, a Charentais on the eleventh, and a Melone Retato on April 16. I'm not sure how to account for these timing differences. Perhaps it's a matter of being a few inches to the right or left on the warming mat or getting a hint more sunshine in one spot than another.

All four of these melons are advertised as heirlooms, but only the French ones came trailing snippets of history. Charentais melons, so the seed catalogs say, date back to the sixteenth century; the Féria du Melon, a two-day festival celebrating them, is still held every July in Cavaillon, a town southeast of Avignon. Petit Gris de Rennes were discovered in the 1600s in the garden of the Bishop of Rennes, in Bretagne. Noir des Carmes are so named because they have very dark green—almost black—rinds, and they were grown by Carmelite monks at least as far back as the 1800s, perhaps even earlier. In contrast, the unlucky Italian melon—whose plain name means "netted melon of gardeners"—comes without any explanation for its heirloom status. But these stories matter. They help us hold on to history, help us care enough to try to keep plants in cultivation, to shield them from extinction. And they teach us about us—about what people cared about enough to cultivate and fine-tune to different climates, about what flavors our forebears found worth preserving. So, with time on my hands and a desire to think about something other than viral transmission rates and COVID-19 symptoms, I set out to learn what I can about Melone Retato, to give it back its story.

Melons, I soon discover, were domesticated thousands of years ago in India and Persia and carried west by traders traveling the Silk Road. During the Roman era, the most common sorts in the Mediterranean region were snake melons and watermelons. In the first century CE, in his *Natural History*, Pliny the Elder described a new melon that was bright yellow and shaped like a quince. It fell off the vine when ripe. Few melons outside the species *Cucumis melo* fall like that, so horticultural historians think Pliny was describing a member of that species, which is the one that Melone Retato Degli Ortolani and the other melons I'm growing all belong to.

C. melo need long warm growing seasons and relatively dry conditions to attain full flavor, warmer and drier even than those in southern Europe. That probably explains why European writers rarely mentioned them during antiquity and the medieval era. Then suddenly, beginning in the late 1400s and on through the next century, references to them abound. Using seeds imported from Armenia, Italian monks were able to grow the sweet melons, and they became a treasured delicacy in Italy.

In fact, they were so loved during the Renaissance that the American botanist Edward Sturtevant wrote, in his compendium *Sturtevant's Edible Plants of the World*, "The admiration of the authors of the sixteenth century for the perfume and exquisite taste of the melon, as contrasted with the silence of the Romans, who were not less epicurean, is assuredly a proof that the melon had not at that time, even if known, attained its present luscious and perfumed properties." While it assuredly is not proof, he's right in a way. Even if the melon Pliny described would have been sweet when fully ripe, Rome didn't have the necessary growing conditions, and warming mats did not yet exist. Emperor Tiberius did have *specularia*, ingenious predecessors to greenhouses. Small garden beds mounted on wheels, they could be placed in the sun on warm, bright days and covered with frames containing semitransparent stone, like mica, when the weather grew cold. However, even with *specularia*, sweet *C. melo* would have been hard to grow.

But during the Renaissance, in the gardens of the popes, the new melons are said to have thrived. Thanks to cross-breeding, the melons had changed enough from their precursors to be considered a separate subspecies, *Cucumis melo* var. *cantalupensis*, the European cantaloupe. We know they were considered a luxury item, one that was popular among the popes. In 1471, when Pope Paul II died, a rumor circulated that his death was due to eating too many melons in a single sitting. And we know what many of those early cantaloupes looked like because in the 1510s, the Renaissance artist Raphael and his assistant, Giovanni Martini da Udine, were commissioned to paint frescoes in the Villa Farnesina in Rome. On the ceiling of one long hall, Raphael created allegorical images of Cupid and Psyche, and his assistant painted vibrant frames around each scene. Creating festoons of greenery studded with fruits, vegetables, and flowers, Giovanni rendered the plants so precisely that horticultural historians have been able to identify 170 distinct species.

Some fruits and vegetables are easy to identify just by their appearance, but doing that with melons is tricky. Many subspecies look similar, and within the same subspecies, fruits grown under different soil and climate conditions can look very different from one another. Adding to the challenge, melons change in appearance quite a bit as they mature. All the same, the frescoes in the villa are a rare and valuable resource; the horticulturalist Jules Janick identified many of the fruits and vegetables depicted there, including four types of *C. melo* var. *cantalupensis*, three from France and one from Algiers. Luckily for me, Janick writes in English and publishes articles for lay audiences as well as specialists.

To my surprise and delight, two of the French melons that Janick recognized, Charentais and Noir des Carmes, are in my garden. None of the melons Janick identified were Italian, which seemed strange to me. Surely an artist like Giovanni Martini da Udine, who was on the rise and beholden to benefactors, would include local cultivars to please his patrons. The omission struck me as so unlikely I decided to take a closer look at the few melons Janick couldn't identify. He'd narrowed them down to being members of the subspecies *C. melo* var. *reticulatus*, which is what Melone Retato is. And one of them looks a lot like it: round, just slightly lobed, netted, with narrow green stripes between the lobes when mature. I won't presume to say a fruit pictured in a JPEG of a five-hundred-year-old painting is definitely a Melone Retato, but it sure looks like one.

The frescoes (may) have expanded Melone Retato's backstory, giving it a pedigree that includes forebears in papal gardens and fancy villas, but they complicated those of Charentais and Noir des Carmes. While seed catalogs routinely emphasize the melons' French connections, they do not mention any Italian roots. And yet, they probably had them. The prominence of the melons we know as Charentais and Noir des Carmes in the frescoes makes far more sense if the paintings depict Italian relatives of the French melons. Plus, melon lore includes the juicy tidbit that King Charles VIII personally brought melon seeds from Italy to France at the end of the fifteenth century. But, like the seed catalog assertion that Melone Retato is an heirloom, most of these mentions of King Charles and melons are brief and vague.

I keep sleuthing.

WHICH IS HOW I learn that around the time King Charles supposedly acquired the seeds, he did, in fact, spend several weeks in Rome. For two of those weeks, he was a guest at the Vatican. There, he saw Pope Alexander VI frequently, though the two were far from friends. Even so, I think the pope probably gave him melon seeds.

A year earlier, the king of Naples had died without a clear line of succession. The young French king had a weak claim to the crown, didn't care that others had stronger claims. When Alfonso II was crowned in May 1494, Charles decided to take the throne by force. He assembled a large army of professional soldiers and mercenaries, and they set out in September of that year, making their way down the Italian peninsula, marauding as they went. Because Naples was a papal fiefdom, King Charles sent a request to Pope Alexander VI, asking for his support in becoming the king of Naples as well as for promises of safe passage through the Catholic-controlled region. When the pope refused, Charles threatened to have him deposed.

Tensions were understandably high when the king and his army reached Rome in late December. Hoping to placate Charles, fearful Roman officials gave him free reign. The pope retreated to the papal fortress to avoid having to interact with the king. But when one of the castle walls collapsed, the pontiff took it as an omen that he must deal with Charles. He reluctantly opened negotiations. On January 15, the pair signed a treaty, its terms highly favorable to the king, who became a guest at the Vatican the next day. The pope and the king met almost every day for the next two weeks.

The pope knew King Charles had been entranced by the Renaissance garden he saw in Florence. Unlike the walled medieval gardens with which Charles was familiar, Renaissance gardens were unwalled and were beautiful as well as useful—with porticoes, columns, and statues arranged amid the flora. By the end of his time in Italy, King Charles was avid about Renaissance gardens, describing one as so nearly perfect that "il semble qu'il n'y faille que Adam et Eve pour en faire une paradis Terrestre," (only Adam and Eve are missing to make it an earthly paradise). Determined to have something similar at his chateau in the Loire Valley, he persuaded twenty-two Italian gardeners and artisans to return with him; they brought many non-native plants to France, including forty orange trees.

Even though it was January, the pope cannily held several of his meetings with the king in the Papal Gardens, including one that was especially private. If Pope Alexander VI did give melon seeds to King Charles VIII, it was during this visit. The two would have exchanged both official and unofficial diplomatic gifts. Custom mostly dictated the official ones, but the unofficial ones would have been just as important to their fraught negotiations. For an ardent botanist, seeds for the melons grown in the Papal Garden would have been a perfect gift. From the pope's perspective, they'd also be perfect; they didn't bear a papal seal, so the king couldn't use them to bolster false claims of the Pope's support.

If only the king had turned around then, gone home to tend his garden. If only he hadn't continued to Naples, I could wrap up this unexpectedly deep dive into the early lives of European cantaloupes right here. Could offer a quick expression of delight that I'd reunited descendants of those early melon kin in my pandemic garden. That would have made a nice, upbeat conclusion to this tale—and I could really use some upbeat conclusions, some feel-good answers. If only I'd gotten that happy ending, what came next might not have happened.

The young king did not turn around. Charles and his army reached Naples in February 1495 and spent not quite six months there before being thoroughly rebuffed. At first, the Neapolitans welcomed them. But as they settled in, the soldiers committed crimes and other acts of depravity, including passing a sexually transmitted disease to Neapolitan prostitutes. The prostitutes infected others, as did the mercenaries, who spread the disease across Europe as they made their ways home. Within five years, *lues venera*, "venereal pestilence," reached epidemic levels in Europe. Over the next fifty years, it reached them worldwide.

Lues venera had no cure, no reliable treatments. Religious and secular leaders throughout Europe rushed to pass ordinances and enact edicts to halt the outbreak. They banned the sick from going out in public, banned those who were ill abroad from returning. But the disease raged on. Frightened and powerless, people blamed their enemies: the French called it "the Neapolitan disease"; Italians and Germans called it "the French disease"; Poles called it "the German disease"; the Dutch called it "the Spanish disease"; Russians called it "the Polish disease."

Then, in 1530, the Italian physician and poet Girolamo Fracastoro published "Syphilis, sive morbus gallicus" ("Syphilis, or the French Disease"). He'd begun writing the poem many years earlier when he was "driven by the plague into the country and had abundant leisure." In his poem, a shepherd named Syphilus displeases the sun god, Apollo, and is punished by being given the disease. Translated, the final line begins, "And after him this malady we call / SYPHILIS."

The name endured.

HOPING TO FIND the story of an Italian melon, I have arrived, unwittingly, at the early days of another pandemic—at the initial outbreak of an awful illness and a long-ago poet's effort to fill his pandemic-induced "leisure" by penning its origin story. That these strands so smoothly intertwine fills me with foreboding: I can't shake the sense that, though peculiar, this strange braid is not unique.

THE LATIN WORD *lues* comes from Lua, who was the Roman goddess of plagues and destruction. Though now considered a minor, obscure goddess, she oversaw two critical realms. She was also a consort to Saturn, the god of agriculture and one of the most important gods in the Roman pantheon. In fact, Lua was his only consort except for his wife, Ops.

Presiding over not one, but two, forms of catastrophe is an odd remit for a minor deity. But maybe Lua wasn't minor or obscure two thousand years ago. Maybe she had an elaborate backstory and cult following, since lost, a pedigree that better explains why she seemed suited to the tasks.

Unlike Saturn and many of the other Roman gods and goddesses, Lua doesn't have a Greek counterpart or an Etruscan precursor. So maybe she was never more than a contour drawing of a goddess, hurriedly created to explain away the inevitable disasters farmers faced. Not only was her lover the god of agriculture, but his wife Ops was goddess of fertility, abundance, and the harvest. Who better to blame than a jealous lover if a farmer's prayers to Ops or Saturn went unanswered?

Or perhaps a pantheon tilted toward creation simply suited young Rome. Maybe a mythology emphasizing growth and expansion, health and harvest, made more sense to an emboldened, empire-building people. Maybe it takes longevity before a culture can see creation and destruction as working in tandem, before it can embrace the inevitability of becoming and being and ceasing to be.

An interview with Buddhist teacher Jack Kornfield appeared in the *New York Times* this week, as the virus ravages the paper's home city. Kornfield said the crazy constellation of feelings that COVID-19 induces are part of our innate fight-or-flight instinct, that emotions are as rooted in our biological being as are the surges of adrenaline we're also experiencing. He suggested we try holding those feelings for a bit, acknowledging them, maybe even say, "Thank you for trying to protect me, but I'm OK."

I want to feel that kind of compassion for my immune system; its tendency to go haywire is a big part of the reason Rob and I are so vigilant. Pathogens that make most people mildly ill can leave me bedridden, and these last few years, since I had cancer, I tend to get even sicker than I did before. If I contract COVID-19, I'm terrified my immune system will set off a cytokine storm and I'll die on a ventilator.

I try to follow Kornfield's guidance, remind myself my body isn't betraying me. To the contrary, it's trying too hard, doing absolutely everything it knows to do to protect me. This reframing doesn't help nearly as much as I'd hoped.

On the plus side, I haven't gotten bronchitis once during lockdown. Nor have I (or most people) gotten the flu. Despite fears among public health officials that we'd have a "twindemic," so far this has been the mildest flu season on record. Even so, experts are already worrying about what could happen in the fall since we'll have less natural immunity to whatever strains are circulating. I'm holding off on borrowing such trouble, trying instead to stay focused on this moment, trying to stay grateful for what isn't.

PRESIDENT TRUMP HAS begun referring to COVID-19 as the "Chinese Flu" and as "Kung Flu" and insists doing so is not racist because the virus originated in China. He won't wear a mask. And last night, he proposed injecting disinfectants to kill the virus: "I see the disinfectant where it knocks it out in a minute, one minute and is there a way we can do something like that by injection inside or almost a cleaning."

What's terrifying is that many people are listening to him. Protesters have started rallying against mask mandates and restrictions on movement and gathering. Some say the government is overreacting, that COVID-19 is no worse than the seasonal flu. Many protestors regard the restrictions as tyrannical: They carry signs saying "freedom to choose," "Don't tread on Me," "Give me liberty or give me Covid-19." How long will it be before someone drinks rubbing alcohol?

I understand that the protesters want life to go back to normal. I want the same thing. But our desires collide. If those who oppose these restrictions move through the world without masks, the coronavirus will spread and mutate, spread and mutate. People like me will have to stay home indefinitely. Those WHO officials who feared that people in liberal democracies would reject the strategies needed to contain the pandemic were right to worry.

PART OF WHAT makes me so frustrated about these protestors is that as far back as the fourth millennium BCE, an era when people believed diseases were punishments from the gods, they still had the good sense to quarantine people who were seriously ill, "confining them to their quarters, letting no one out and no one in." Even without the benefit of germ theory, they exercised restraint to protect themselves and others. But now, when we know how diseases spread, a shocking number of people still balk at having any constraints.

I keep thinking about Hannah Arendt, who wrote often and eloquently about the natures of freedom and authoritarianism and their connections to ethics. People who are free, she wrote, are able "to move, to get away from home, to go out into the world and meet other people in word and deed," all things we cannot do right now. But even as she extolled the freedom of movement, Arendt didn't say it ought to be absolute. To the contrary, she considered a public emergency the one instance when truly free people must stop acting "as equals among equals" and instead start "commanding and obeying one another."

ONE HUNDRED DAYS ago, the first person in the US tested positive for the coronavirus. That's all, just one hundred days ago. A hint more than three months. Since then, over a million people here have had it, more than three million worldwide. And more than twenty-six million people in the US filed for unemployment this month, a less horrifying statistic, yes, but terrible and terrifying in its own way.

IT'S HARD TO believe May is just days away. Yesterday, it snowed again, the fourth time in as many weeks. And I found myself intoning T. S. Eliot's famous line, "April is the cruellest month." Such Eliot-quoting is usually the purview of harried English majors, but this month it's been surprisingly widespread, with newscasters, headline writers, and regular people pointing out how apt Eliot's words are to the out-of-kilter-ness of pandemic spring. And no wonder: Eliot knew what of.

When Eliot called April cruel, he wasn't complaining about late snow; the whole sentence, the first in his poem "The Waste Land," reads: "April is the cruellest month breeding / Lilacs out of the dead land, mixing / Memory and desire, stirring / Dull roots with spring rain." To him, what was cruel about April was not that the plants were on hold but precisely the opposite. While lilacs and other plants were coming back to life, humans were stuck in a limbo. One of his characters said, "I could not / Speak, and my eyes failed, I was neither / Living nor dead." People in his waste land could remember what their lives used to be like and could hope that some version of normalcy would eventually return, but they were mostly powerless to bring about change.

Literary critics often say, rightly, that "The Waste Land" offers social commentary about the bleakness of Europe after World War I. But that war was coupled with another catastrophe. In 1918, much of the world endured two waves of the Spanish flu. When the first wave ended in Great Britain during the summer, the English thought the epidemic was behind them. Then, in October, a second, far deadlier wave arrived; those who contracted it had high fevers, headaches, weakness, achiness, joint pain, and heavy coughing. Those whose lungs filled with fluid soon suffocated to death. The more virulent strain roiled the world over the next many months.

Researchers believe that flu virus probably emerged in China during the winter of 1917–18 and was carried to other countries by members of the Chinese Labour Corps. Worldwide, outbreaks began among the military, as troops were crowded together in encampments and trenches, on trains and transport ships. Servicemen carried the disease from place to place, eventually bringing it home when the war ended. The Spanish flu hit countries already suffering war losses especially hard, adding to the surreal grief survivors faced. The war-dead were absent; without the bodies of soldiers lost in battle to inter, families and friends had to accept their losses without the chance for a ritual goodbye. In contrast, those who died from the Spanish flu were all too present. When the number of dead exceeded a community's ability to bury them, bodies literally piled up. Those are the dead, I think, whom Eliot described as a huge ghostly crowd flowing "over London Bridge, so many, / I had not thought death had undone so many."

T. S. Eliot and his first wife, Vivienne, both contracted the Spanish flu in December, soon after the war ended. In a letter to her brother shortly after Armistice was declared, Vivienne said she was so worn out from being sick that she had "not been able to rejoice much over Peace! In the abstract I do, and I try to make myself *realize it*. But conditions here will be so hard, harder than *ever*, perhaps, for a long, long time, and I must say it *is* difficult to feel anything at all. One is too stunned altogether."

LIKE MANY WARRING nations, Great Britain censored newspapers and prohibited references to the influenza outbreaks. Spain—which remained neutral during the war—didn't censor, so people learning of the disease from Spanish sources assumed, incorrectly, that the illness originated there, which is how it became known as Spanish flu. Others attributed it to enemies, as happened with syphilis; some referred to the flu as "Naples Soldier," "Russian Pest," "Chinese flu," or "Flanders fever."

When the second outbreak arrived in Great Britain, politicians and press urged people to adopt assorted measures to avoid getting sick. Some recommended drinking milk or whiskey, others eating onions or porridge or sugary treats. Some thought cigarette smoking would prevent infection. Some doctors advised taking thirty grams of aspirin, not realizing the dosage could be lethal. Their most sensible suggestions are among those heard again today: Be outdoors as much as possible. Make sure indoor spaces are well ventilated. Wear masks. Practice good hygiene.

But as the caseload continued into the winter, British politicians tried to downplay the danger, reluctant to further overwhelm the exhausted public with more bad news. A public health recommendation to avoid large crowds and stay home if sick was "buried by the government." In this news vacuum, conspiracy theories took hold; an article in the *Sussex Daily News* proposed the outbreak was "an ingenious attempt" to "sabotage the forthcoming general election." By late 1919, when the third wave of Spanish flu abated, 228,000 people had died from it in England alone. Between the devastation of the war and that of the flu, the country lost much of its international standing; the British Empire began to wane. Around the world, the effects of the Spanish flu were similarly dire: Half a billion people, one-third of everyone, were infected. At least fifty million people, 5 percent of the world's population, died. This is the pandemic whose "sinister path" the WHO fears COVID-19 may follow.

WHEN THE SPANISH flu reached Maine in late September 1918, it surged for two months. Some residents bristled at the state-ordered closures and other restrictions; several Catholic priests, for example, argued the government order to close churches violated their freedom of worship. But after interviewing many survivors, a local historian noted neither the flu nor the regulations undercut peoples' sense of community: "Even though the influenza epidemic touched every family," he wrote, "it left the social fabric as a whole unchanged." He quoted one survivor who recalled feeling "there was a closeness about it," that "people really cared about each other. We were working together because of the war, and then we were working together because of the flu."

Before the 1918 flu outbreak, each municipality in Maine had its own local health officer and its own board of health; they didn't report to any statewide authority. In 1919, after seeing the array of community responses to the epidemic—ranging from closures and mask mandates, on the one hand, to no recommendations by public officials, on the other—the state legislature gave the Maine Department of Health authority to issue recommendations and health guidance and charged local health officers with reporting all health threats to that department.

LIKE OUR TOWN'S elected officials, the local health officer is publicly silent about COVID-19. I'm confounded by—and angry about—this. In the absence of medicine, knowledge is the only possible panacea. And while it's inspiring that folks in our task force work to stay abreast of what's happening and to distill the swirl of information into helpful materials for the community, it's beyond maddening that the elected and appointed folks who are supposed to lead us won't. During one of our weekly Zooms with state public health folks, Kate and I learn such inaction isn't unique, that many local health officers, town managers, and select boards are remaining publicly mum.

SIX OR SEVEN Tahiti daffodils are in bloom, and the tamaracks are starting to green. The spinach, on the other hand, remains pallid, almost yellow. I'm sure it's sun-starved. But in case it's also hankering for nitrogen or other nutrients, I give it a hefty dose of stinky fish emulsion.

MAY

YESTERDAY, MAY 1, Maine's governor eased the lockdown requirements slightly; now, salons, barbershops, and pet groomers can reopen—not that we'll be availing ourselves of any of them until the pandemic abates. My hair is long enough now that I need barrettes or a hairband. Rob's superfine hair is no longer a flattop; it's beginning to flop. He ordered hair clippers during the first week of lockdown, and they arrived at last, so I give him a haircut. We do it outside, with him sitting on the stone wall. I buzz and clip away the excess until he has something akin to a #5 fade, leaving the shorn bits on the wall and lawn for birds to take for their nests.

THE LOOSENING OF lockdown rules doesn't mean the pandemic is subsiding. The number of confirmed COVID-19 cases continues to rise. Worldwide, cases exceeded 3,338,000; in the US, they surpassed 1,101,000, a third of all reported cases. I struggle not to let that fact deepen my despair.

WORKING IN THE greenhouse helps push the gloom aside, at least for a little while. My gardening tasks at this time of the season are easy and repetitive. Today, I'm potting up, which entails taking the healthiest seedlings from the seed trays and replanting them in four-inch pots. Six Peach Melba nasturtiums, six Mr. Majestic double marigolds, eleven tomatoes, and a dozen Row 7 cucumbers are all now in roomier quarters. Potting up happens in batches, as seedlings are ready at different rates. But within a month, all the plants should be in their final spots.

Though we're officially six weeks into spring, few plants in the yard are in leaf, even fewer in flower. A smattering of violets dots the mulch by the stewartia tree. Nearby, furred fern caps push through the topsoil. The tamaracks are budding. Red-brown nodules stipple their branches. In days, the outermost arc of each will be breached by a bristle of yellow-green needle tips. And in less than a week, the daffodils will come on strong, with dozens arriving each day—an array of yellows, peaches, oranges, creams, and whites, some with flecks of gold.

ROB PREPPED THE potato beds for me yesterday, broad forking them and adding compost. So today, I'm hoping to get all the potatoes planted. Like most growers, I start potatoes not from seeds but from seed potatoes, tubers saved from the previous season's harvest. We use seed potatoes because potatoes do not grow "true"; their seeds contain so much genetic diversity that their offspring may be wildly different from the parent. But the offspring of seed potatoes are clones, identical to the parent. Able to reproduce both sexually and asexually, potatoes have benefitted from the strengths each strategy offers.

We don't have a root cellar, so I can't save my own potatoes to grow. Instead, I buy them from a woman whose small business specializes in Maine potatoes. When the potatoes arrive, I put them in a shallow box in the pass-through to "chit," or sprout. Each of the tiny eyes will grow nubby sprouts. Ideally, I'll plant them before the sprouts get too large, as they'll fall off if they become long and spindly. Chitting isn't essential, but the potatoes begin to leaf sooner if they've had time to presprout.

To plant potatoes, I scoop out a row-long trench, then cut several seed potatoes into pieces, making sure each has at least one eye or sprout. I plant the pieces a foot apart, cut side down, then mound the row with compost and more loam, lightly patting the mixture into place before repeating the process for the rest of the eight pounds of seed potatoes.

The surface of the bed swells and subsides, like gently corrugated metal. My handprints on the domed dirt remind me of the hand marks on the walls and ceilings in prehistoric cave paintings. Those are mostly red or black or ochre; some are outlines, others fully painted in. In some caves the handprints are by themselves, but my prints on the potato hills make me think of the dozens of reddish, overlapping handprints in the Cave of the Hands in Argentina. No one knows what the painters meant in making them; researchers can't even agree on whether they were made by young men or grown women. Whoever they were, I bet one of their messages was simply, "I was here."

Unlike those ancient cave markings, my handprints disappear in a day or two. Where they'd been, cracks appear in about a week. Beneath those cracks, still out of sight, nascent leaves unsettle the soil, push it away as they force themselves skyward. The cracks are a signal from the potatoes-to-come—"We're almost here."

WE HAVE FOUR varieties of potatoes: Red Norland, Magic Molly, La Ratte, and Katahdin. Growing them is a delicious pleasure, a way to have fresher and more varied tubers than I can find in stores or at the farmers market. And this year, it's taken on more significance, as the massive layoffs and broken supply chains have made finding specific groceries hard. Once a week, Rob goes shopping. Sometimes, he finds what we want; other times, he settles for something similar, or we do without. The trips are frustrating and stressful. After each stop, he sits in his truck, takes off his mask, cleans his hands, wipes down the door handles and steering wheel, cleans his credit card, re-cleans his hands, and redons his mask. While he's gone, I set up a cleaning area in the kitchen; when he gets home, he wipes down the groceries with a weak bleach solution before we put them away.

We are supplementing what we get from conventional stores and the food co-op with a community supported agriculture share. This early in the growing season, the CSA share is mostly fresh greens and storing vegetables harvested last fall. The farmers have welcomed newcomers into the CSA, for which I'm grateful, but they didn't know last year that they'd have so many new customers this spring. Their reserve of carrots and parsnips and turnips is being quickly depleted. Knowing we'll have homegrown food from midsummer until December is a relief.

THE RED NORLANDS are an early season potato; they'll be ready by mid-July. They have dark-red skin and bright-white flesh. Raw, they're so firm they crunch like cider apples. Even before the plants die back, which is the sign potatoes are ready to be harvested, we'll grabble a few, carefully burrowing under a plant by hand and gently tugging some potatoes from the roots.

La Ratte and Magic Molly, both fingerlings, will be ready next, probably in late July or early August. La Ratte grow in a pale-beige tangle like a nest of baby mice, so I thought (wrongly) that their name came from "rat." The potatoes grow so close together that they're like living puzzle pieces; their shapes counterpoint their neighbors as they curve to accommodate each other. Magic Molly potatoes are much larger than La Ratte and don't grow in a tight tangle. Their special attribute is color. Molly skins are purply-brown, and their flesh is intensely purple; they hold their hue when cooked.

Katahdin, named for Maine's highest mountain, is a slightly prolate storing potato with tan skin and white flesh. We leave them in the ground until the plants have totally died back, then store them inside in a dark, cool spot. They usually keep into December, occasionally into January. Katahdin are a cross between two USDA potato germ lines that never got commercial names, are still known only as #40568 and #24642. It's technically native to Maine, having been created at a research station in northern Aroostook County in 1932, but calling it "native" seems an overreach to me since the researchers could as easily have crossed #40568 and #24642 in some other state. True Mainers wouldn't bother with such cavil, would bluntly point out that Katahdin potatoes are not native, that "just because a cat has her kittens in the oven don't make them biscuits."

DIFFERENT AS THEY are from one another, the four kinds of potatoes we're growing all have the same ancient forebear. Early agriculturalists in the Andean highlands of South America began domesticating wild potatoes at least eight thousand years ago, and a single kind of potato from near Lake Titicaca is thought to be the "primary ancestor" of all domesticated potatoes. Whereas humans benefitted from domesticating cereals by generating larger yields of the domesticated versions, they benefitted from domesticating wild potatoes by making versions that were less poisonous. Wild potatoes contain solanine and tomatine, two toxins that aren't neutralized by heat, so they remain troublesome even after potatoes are cooked. Consuming these compounds can cause gastrointestinal distress and neurological problems. Somehow, early Andean growers figured out that dipping the potatoes in edible clay made them safe to eat. The clay binds with the toxins, so they move through the body without being absorbed; even now, eating potatoes with clay sauce is common in the highlands.

Over time, ancient Andeans bred more than a thousand nontoxic potato varieties, fitting them to different altitudes, cooking methods, and taste preferences. Peruvian farmers continue to cultivate so many kinds of potatoes that environmental scientist Karl Zimmerer said a single potato field in the Andes has more diversity than 90 percent of the potato crop grown in the United States. Contemporary Peruvian potatoes are visually even more different from each other than Magic Molly is from Katahdin. They are long and short, fat and thin; some are "conical, round, kidney-shaped, coiled—even concertina shaped. Colors range from white to black, with all shades of red, yellow and blue in between; in a variety of patterns: spotted, striped, splashed, spectacled and stippled."

WHEN OUR ANCESTORS began domesticating plants, they changed more than their diets. They reshaped ecosystems to encourage the plants they wanted and discourage the plants they didn't. They also began to domesticate wild animals, turning them into livestock. As the early farmers expanded the area they cultivated, converting wilderness into farmland, they encountered insects carrying unfamiliar diseases. Likewise, when they domesticated goats and sheep and chickens and other animals, they were exposed to bacteria and viruses that coevolved with those animals. And because the farmers and animals were staying put, their waste accumulated, creating ideal environments for insects and microorganisms to thrive.

Historians and epidemiologists attribute human pandemics to the invention of farming. Today, 60 percent of diseases humans have are "zoonotic," meaning they originated in animals other than humans. Even so, I find myself resisting the assertion that "if it weren't for agriculture we wouldn't have pandemics," looking for ways to prove it wrong. At first, I thought my visceral reaction to this notion was because I'm so invested in the idea of my garden being a pandemic corrective. I wanted the historians to be wrong because I want my garden—my little agricultural patch—to be a living rejoinder to the pandemic, a beautiful, vibrant, snippy clapback.

But the more I think about the connection folks draw between agriculture and pandemics, the more I believe it truly is an oversimplification. Some epidemics happened before the invention of agriculture, including terrible malaria outbreaks. And early agriculturalists were unlikely to have been super-spreaders. If a virus jumped from a sheep to a person in those early years, it could kill the farmer or even the entire community, but it would die along with them unless a new host happened by.

Rather than "agriculture led to pandemics," I think it'd be more accurate to say something like "farming helped prime the world for pathogen spread." Early farmers would rarely have carried pathogens to faraway places. But eventually, people became good enough at growing food that some community members could do something other than farm. People could cultivate other arts and interests. As that happened, communities grew larger, towns emerged, then cities. New power structures arose, with rulers who wanted to protect their property and seize more territory; they'd conscript soldiers to accomplish both. Those with means purchased items they could not produce for themselves, and trade expanded. Exotic goods moved between regions, as caravans traveled along trade routes selling luxuries.

Cities, trade, and soldiers—no less than domesticated plants and animals—are agricultural products.

THEY'RE ALSO SUPERB disease-transmission vectors. Few early towns or cities solved the problem of managing waste; as on farms, human and animal waste in urban areas provided breeding ground for pathogens. And most urban people lived in cramped, close quarters, ensuring new hosts for the pathogens. Urbanites were also exposed to novel pathogens carried by traders and soldiers from abroad. The Axumite salt trade route, the Persian Royal Road, and the Sabaean Way, as well as the later and better-known Spice Road and Silk Road, were major cultural developments, shuttling foods, luxury items, and pathogens from place to place.

Over time, as the ethnobotanist Gary Paul Nabhan noted, what began as bartering—exchanging the heady spices native to arid regions for foods that wouldn't grow there—became something else entirely: "The spice trade triggered an economic and ecological revolution that rippled out to every reach of the human-inhabited world. It is the revolution that we now call globalization." Trade has morphed well beyond exchanging spices for staples, beyond giving aristocrats access to exotica. Now, many tons of goods move across the world each day, an exchange network that's facilitating the spread of the coronavirus.

Likewise, soldiers carried pathogens beyond their natural borders. Early militaries were comprised of conscripted farmers who fought during the agricultural offseason. I imagine that when those soldiers saw novel cultivars that were thriving, they brought some home at battle's end. They wouldn't mean to carry germs along for the ride, wouldn't know they were doing so.

When Alexander the Great conquered the region from Persia to the Indus Valley in northwest India, he and his army gathered scores of plants they then introduced to Europe. In India, Alexander's troops saw sugarcane for the first time; one awed officer noted the locals could make honey without bees by using this "honey-bearing reed." They were also amazed by shrubs bearing tufts of "vegetable wool," or cotton, that the "natives made into garments of surpassing whiteness" and used as bedding. Aristotle—the same Aristotle who delineated virtue ethics—asked Alexander, who had been his student, to please conquer the island of Socotra so the Greeks could have easy access to a species of aloe growing there. The philosopher-botanist Theophrastus, another of Aristotle's students, made the more modest request that Alexander give him samples of any interesting plants he brought home.

Militaries also carried their preferred plants with them into new territories. As the Roman Empire expanded north-ward, for example, soldiers brought the foods they liked with them, along with whatever pathogens accompanied the chick-peas, figs, olives, leeks, and other items the men didn't want to live without.

WHEN WE MOVED to our current place, a new neighbor welcomed us to the road with Siberian iris bulbs thinned from her own. A friend gave us seeds for purple lupine with a special backstory, another a self-renewing handful of poppy seeds. Still others bestowed a pair of dainty antique rosebushes and some hellebores. The gift givers all live in Maine and the gifts all came from Maine, but the forebears for all those plants came from Alexander the Great's ancient empire.

THOUGH IT'S WARM enough now that I sit outside to drink my morning coffee, few of those floral gifts are in bloom. But we do have speckles and splashes of color. The tamaracks' needles are an almost neon shade of chartreuse that the evergreens nearby will never attain. Apple leaves no bigger than my pinkie fingernail furl in on themselves, the same pale green as the clumps of *Usnea* swaying from the tree's gray-brown branches. The serviceberries' leaves are opening, their undersides rust-colored, their tops nearer to red. Their proper name is *Amelanchier*; they got the common name serviceberry because when they bloom, the ground is soft enough to dig graves and inter the remains of those who died during the winter. This is the kind of local lore I love. But this spring, as the *Amelanchier* awaken and the ground grows soft, I think about the rows of refrigerator trucks serving as makeshift morgues in New York City and other pandemic hot spots, about the bodies who won't be buried any time soon, about the grieving families waiting indefinitely for the rituals of closure.

Amid the spruces, I glimpse flecks of white: the plum tree is starting to flower. So, too, is the single crimson azalea sitting among yet more spruces on an outcropping of rock a few feet from my spot in the morning sun. The other flowering trees are slower to reach showiness. The apple and crab apple flowers are still weeks away. The stewartia and hawthorn trail them. The lilac cones are shapelier now than at the beginning of the month, though their flowers remain stubbornly closed. The lily of the valley pips are beginning to pop, tight nubs opening into white bells. According to legend, when lily of the valley blooms, happiness returns. We'll see. Spring has returned at last, so there's that.

The crows have also returned, several so big I'd swear they were ravens. They caw as they play in the spruce trees, chasing each other up a branch or down two, screeching to dissuade little birds from lingering. Robins own the lawn, still winter-faded in places, but now more green than tan. On the north side, in the high branches of a spruce spared last spring when its neighbors fell, a bald eagle often perches. His home is elsewhere, but he stops by regularly. During the workweek, I can hear the thrumming motors of lobster boats; even if I can't see them, I know when the captains bait their pots by the frantic squawks and screams of swarming gulls.

A hummingbird flits from one *Camassia* spike to the next. Little birds linger among the kiwi vines; come fall, they'll eat most of the grape-sized fruits before they're ripe enough for people. Bigger birds will peck the apples, fret them to expose moist flesh. After the apples fall, wild turkeys eat whatever the other critters have rejected. Unlike the human world, that of the birds seems entirely unchanged.

"THE TEACHERS ARE struggling," Beckie says on our weekly task force Zoom, meaning the teachers at the town's K–8 school.

She asks if there's anything we can do for them. Someone suggests we make them masks, which, I will admit, does not strike me as particularly uplifting. Then Linda says the sewing group at her church would surely help, and I realize lots of people are probably craving ways to be useful and kind. Plus, whether the teachers love the masks or not, they need them. And the best kind, N95s, are impossible to find. So I agree to locate some fabric featuring dragons, the school mascot, if someone else will organize the volunteers. In less than a day, ten women have offered to do the sewing.

Online, I find lots of dragon-adorned fabrics—cute pastel cartoony dragons, bold-hued fire breathers, noble creatures suited to heraldic shields. Already, the sellers have added information about which fabrics will work for face masks. When everything arrives, I make little kits with cloth, braided elastic for ear loops, and sewing directions, and put them in a harvest hod on the front porch. The volunteers empty the hod, then refill it over the next two weeks with masks, seventy-eight in all, more than enough for everyone who works at the school.

THE SCHOOLS ARE still shuttered to reduce virus transmission, but so far, grammar school age children aren't getting nearly as sick as adults. Usually, children are more affected by respiratory viruses, so this aberration is one of the few sources of solace.

In 430 BCE, when an epidemic ravaged Athens, something similar happened. Athens was then home to around seventy-five thousand people, with another two hundred to two hundred fifty thousand who lived in the surrounding countryside of Attica. Under normal circumstances, the Athenians would have been enjoying the peace and prosperity of their Golden Age, a century of well-being that was then peaking during the rule of Pericles. Intellectual and artistic creativity was high: The ideas of the moral philosopher Socrates were being presented in dialogues by his student Plato. Sophocles and Euripides were writing tragedies, many of which have survived; the Acropolis and Parthenon were built. Athens then was a heady place.

But in 431 BCE, Athens and Sparta went to war. Seeking safety behind the city's wall, the residents of rural Attica moved into Athens. With so many new arrivals, conditions quickly became unsanitary. Even so, when a plague arrived the following year, comparatively few young children became sick. Given the high infant mortality rate and the poor living conditions, their apparent immunity is amazing. Other epidemics of that era killed children in large numbers, but this one spared infants and toddlers—at least during its first wave.

In his *History of the Peloponnesian War*, Thucydides offers a grim list of symptoms for the Plague of Athens: "People in good health were all of a sudden attacked by violent heats in the head, and redness and inflammation in the eyes, the inward parts, such as the throat or tongue, becoming bloody and emitting an unnatural and fetid breath. These symptoms were followed by sneezing and hoarseness." Those flu-like symptoms were followed by a bout of digestive system woes and the eruption of "small pustules and ulcers" all over the body.

"They perished in wild disorder," Thucydides wrote. "Bodies of dying men lay one upon the other, and half-dead people rolled about in the streets and, in their longing for water, near all the fountains." Losing hope as the plague wore on, "men, not knowing what was to become of them, became utterly careless of everything, whether sacred or profane"; they grew lawless and "coolly ventured on what they had formerly done in a corner."

The plague killed weak and strong, rich and poor. Caregivers routinely caught it and died alongside their patients. In recognizing that link, Thucydides was one of the first people to say diseases could be transmitted from one person to another. Coming in waves, the plague lasted five years, during which two of Pericles's sons, his daughter, his wife, and Pericles himself all died. It likely killed a hundred thousand Athenians, a third of the residents of the city-state, and brought the Golden Age of Athens to an end.

CENTURIES LATER, A legend arose that the Greek physician Hippocrates single-handedly saved the rest of Greece from the infection by building bonfires around Athens to cleanse the unhealthy air—though there's no record of him either treating plague victims or building said bonfires (which would not, in fact, have affected a cure). But Hippocrates did transform medicine.

He was the first physician in the Western world to attribute illnesses to natural causes rather than supernatural ones. He thought bodily fluids regulated well-being and that having the right ratio of blood, phlegm, yellow bile, and black bile was essential. In "The Nature of Man," Hippocrates wrote that "health is primarily that state in which these constituent substances are in the correct proportion to each other, both in strength and quantity, and are well mixed. Pain occurs when one of the substances presents either a deficiency or an excess or is separated in the body and not mixed with others."

The balance among the fluids wasn't strictly internal; it could be influenced by external changes related to season, temperature, weather, and location. Recognizing that well-being involved an interplay of inner and outer conditions, Hippocrates emphasized eating wisely to prevent or cure diseases. Among the foods he promoted, onions ranked high. Hippocrates considered them as much a medicine as a food, believing they could cure an array of ailments ranging from constipation to fluid retention to flesh wounds. Likewise, Pliny the Elder thought onions could alleviate insomnia, venereal diseases, dog bites, and poor eyesight.

Natural philosophers weren't the only ones who admired the therapeutic qualities of onions. Olympic athletes of that era believed onions enhanced strength and endurance and balanced the blood. When preparing for competition, they ate pounds of onions, drank onion juice, and rubbed onion paste on their bodies. In fact, when Socrates described onions as primarily a relish, one of his companions chided him, saying, "Heaven forbid, Socrates! . . . When a man is setting out for battle, it is well for him to nibble an onion, just as some people give their gamecocks a feed of garlic before pitting them together in the ring."

BY THE TIME Hippocrates hailed onions and Socrates gave them short shrift, both wild and domesticated onions had become staples in human diets. Hundreds of wild members of the

Allium family grew throughout the world, and the large bulb onion, *Allium cepa*, or common onion, had been domesticated in
the Fertile Crescent twenty-five hundred years earlier. Thanks to
the survival of several cuneiform tablets from Babylon, we know
recipes for dozens of dishes eaten there. In addition to bulb onions, leeks and garlic figure prominently among the ingredients.

Domesticated onions were carried to the Middle East by
traders and then made their way to other continents, where
they were warmly welcomed. Onions have much to recommend
them: they are easy to grow, easy to store, can be eaten raw or
cooked, and provide nutrients and strong flavors that augment
bland cereal-based diets. In the Americas, Indigenous peoples
ate many wild alliums. Domesticated onions arrived with European colonizers; Christopher Columbus brought onions and
garlic to Hispaniola, while British colonists introduced them to
kitchen gardens in New England.

EVERY YEAR, I grow chives and scallions and garlic, as well as
one or two kinds of bulb onions—usually copras and cipollinis.
Copras are hard yellow onions that store well and rarely grow
much bigger than my fist; cipollinis are smaller, flatter, and
sweeter, the perfect onions for grilling. We often harvest sixty
pounds or more of the bulb onions. That's not enough to last us
until the next year, but even copras won't make it that long. We
usually run out around the time they start to soften and sprout.

Onions have a long growing season; it takes eight to ten
weeks for the seeds to produce seedlings large enough to
plant outdoors, and in our region, the ideal time to transplant

seedlings is mid- to late-April. So I buy starts instead. Sold in bunches, they look like sheaves of miniature scallions with very hairy roots. Since these are live plants, customers let on-line retailers know when they'd like them to arrive. This year, the delay-bedeviled postal service delivered ours on May 10. Having languished in transit for so long, the onions couldn't be revived—and the company I'd ordered them from was long since sold out.

I couldn't find copras anywhere, but a vendor in Texas still had cipollinis; I crossed my fingers and bought some. Both co-pras and cipollinis are "long-day onions," which means they require fourteen to sixteen hours of sunlight per day to begin bulbing. In Texas, short-day onions do better, so I wasn't sure how well cipollinis started there would fare here. I needn't have worried: almost every start reached maturity, and their Texan roots may explain why they were the largest, tangiest cippolini I've ever seen or eaten.

WHEN I CUT onions, I cry. Not just misty eyes and a few sniffs, but full-on rolling-down-my-cheeks, pebble-sized tears. So lately, when I grow paranoid that a sore throat or achy feel-ing is an early COVID-19 symptom, I sniff an onion. Smelling it reassures me that I probably don't have the virus, since an in-ability to smell and taste things, "anosmia," has been widely re-ported by people who've gotten sick. Doctors don't know why folks lose their sense of smell, but it happens a lot. Some people who became ill in February and March have reported regaining their senses of smell and taste, but many haven't.

I would hate that. I'd miss the tastes and smells of food, of course, but I think I'd miss the smells of the garden and yard even more. When I walk by a rosemary or lavender plant, I nearly always gather a spike or two in my hand, tug upward gently to let its fragrance gather on my fingers. I brush my hands across herbs and evergreens to summon their scents. Even unpleasant smells can be oddly gratifying: I have a love-hate relationship with the reek tomato plants leave on my hands when I prune them, a tangy scent redolent of urine and soil and freshly cut grass.

Like the garden, the yard produces a gorgeous jumble of smells. Warming, wet soil in mud season; late spring lilacs, some so intensely sweet I don't bring their branches inside; dusky low-bush blueberry plants on hot days; freshly cut grass; a carpet of ochre pine needles; moldering leaves. Technically, I could live without a sense of smell, but losing it would sever one of the more exquisite tethers between my body and this place.

NOW THAT IT'S late May, part of my garden work is hardening off. Each morning, I carry seedlings outside, leave them there for a few hours, then bring them back into the greenhouse. Each successive day, they stay outside a little longer before going back inside by evening. Yesterday, they were ready to stay out overnight, though today I'm bringing them back inside; I think they need one more day and night in their containers before I start planting them in the ground. This incremental exposure lets the young plants adjust to real world conditions after their cozy start indoors. If I planted them outside without first hardening them off, most would die, too delicate to endure the harsh conditions the world can inflict.

ON MAY 25, in Minneapolis, a forty-six-year-old man Black named George Floyd was murdered by a white police officer who knelt on his neck until he stopped breathing. Protestors have taken to the streets, not just in Minnesota, but all over the country.

Unable to participate, I pay attention from home. Even from a distance, I can sense some differences between these vigils and marches and past demonstrations. Many more people are protesting. More politicians are taking a knee alongside protestors. The protestors are more racially diverse than is often the case. Within days, the protests extend to other countries. I think the pandemic may be playing a part in raising awareness, stoking fury. I hope it is. The ubiquitous virus is giving many people their first intimations of existential terror, something Black Americans know far too well. Around the world, people are absorbing the stark fact that a chance encounter or a momentary lapse in vigilance could cost them their lives. I want to believe such knowledge fosters empathy, want it to persist after the pandemic abates.

JUNE

❦ ❦

ON JUNE 4, the weather is so beautiful, I overdo it, get my first sunburn of the season while weeding the wild-flower bed.

THE ACUTE CRAVING for color I'd felt in early spring has abated, though I still take pleasure in the arrival of each new hue. Since I can't travel, I'm trying to more fully appreciate that we live amid an ever-changing landscape. The lilacs in the side yard—white and pale lavender and deep purple—are unusual-ly prolific. The creamy cones of horse chestnut flowers are in bloom. And the first round of *Rosa rugosa* blooms have arrived, some white, most magenta. Pale purple and white irises stand erect and prim beneath an unruly sweep of tamarack, their pale green needles encroaching on an adjacent bayberry. By the swale, the Siberian irises from our neighbor bloom for the first time—the deep, royal purple all the more satisfying for its unexpectedness. I try to love the rhododendrons our predecessor here must have adored, the many shapely shrubs of gaudy flowers—pale pink, bubblegum, rose, cerise, carmine.

Being surrounded by such lush beauty feels almost unseemly given the bleakness of the wider world. The pandemic hasn't abated at all; as of yesterday, there were over 6.7 million cases and nearly four hundred thousand deaths. And the protests in the wake of George Floyd's killing are growing. My niece Ciara went to a Black Lives Matter rally, which surprised me only because she and her family—my brother Brian's family—live in Ireland. I'm awash in conflicting feelings: proud that Ciara participated, amazed that so many protests of George Floyd's murder are happening internationally, fearful she may have caught COVID-19, not too pleased that she violated Dublin's super-strict lockdown (without her parents' knowledge, no less). Mostly, though, I feel cautiously hopeful. Seventeen years old and an ocean away, Ciara senses how important it is to decry this crime—and she's but one of the many, many thousand protesters the world over insisting that we say his name.

THE LATE-NIGHT COMEDIANS are back from hiatus. Last night, Stephen Colbert opened his monologue saying he never imagined "a global pandemic would not be the lead story. Remember when we were all afraid of our groceries? I miss those days. No, the story that has pushed a hundred thousand COVID deaths below the fold is America's preexisting condition: racism."

THOUGH I DIDN'T anticipate the Black Lives Matter protests would cross the ocean, I should have. Much like seeds and viruses, ideas can spread beyond their homeplaces if carried by human hosts. When ideas reach a congenial environment, they can thrive, reproduce, spread further. When they arrive in an unwelcoming milieu, they often die. The writer William S. Burroughs proposed that language, the genetic material of ideas, is not merely *like* a virus, but that it *is* a virus. This provocative claim would probably have gotten a lot more attention if he hadn't also said the language-virus came from outer space. The language-virus uses people for its own ends: we propagate language, spread it wherever we go. Burroughs points to that as proof of his claim, says language "clearly bears the single identifying feature of a virus: it is an organism with no internal function other than to replicate itself." Had Burroughs lived into the age of social media, he'd likely have felt vindicated. Now, people routinely describe both verbal and visual memes as going viral.

If language is a virus, it's not just any sort of virus; it's a retrovirus. Viruses work by breaking open cells and taking over their replication mechanisms to make more of themselves, but retroviruses don't stop there. They insert their genomes into the host's DNA so that going forward, the host's genome includes some of the virus's. So many retroviruses infected our ancestors that half the human genome, the elegant double helix that codes us, is comprised of genes from ancient viruses (the ordinary, earthly sort). Most of those ancient viral bits don't appear to do much. However, some sequences are functional and quite important. At least a few have helped to make us human.

Around 150 million years ago, a retrovirus entered the egg

of some egg-laying vertebrate. Later, when the egg was fertilized, the baby whatever-it-was grew inside an eggshell, walled off from the world until it was ready to hatch. During that time, the baby got its nutrients from a source inside the egg, just as a baby chick relies on an egg's yolk for food until it hatches.

That ancient critter differed from its predecessors because the retrovirus altered its genome. Rather than the change harming the host, the viral genes gave the critter a new ability: it was able to synthesize syncytin, a protein that can fuse to itself. Imagine silicone tape, only better. As the progeny of the critter with the virus-laden DNA evolved, the mother and the fetus collaboratively turned that plane of protein into a sac, one they fused to the inner wall of the mother's uterus: the sac became the placenta. This new organ served as both a wall, separating the baby and its blood from the mother, and a lifeline, letting nutrients reach the fetus and shuttling waste materials out. Instead of developing in an eggshell outside the mother's body, the embryo could develop inside the mother, vastly improving its odds of surviving until birth. Little wonder this placental adaptation spread widely. An entirely new class of viviparous animals emerged: mammals.

If that retrovirus hadn't invaded some ancient egg, maybe mammals would still have evolved, eventually. Or maybe not.

I THINK THE placenta is the most awesome product of an invading virus getting domesticated, but it's far from the only one. Humans contain more microbial cells than human cells—more, in fact, than there are stars in the universe. Going strictly by the numbers, we're symbionts like lichen, rife with microbial refinements, alliances, and outsourcing agreements.

Microbes that dwell in the uterus, for example, help fertilized eggs develop. The transformations that happen as a human zygote divides again and again on its way to becoming a baby are guided by both microbial and human genes. Science writer Ed Yong describes this embryonic development as "the result of an ongoing negotiation—a conversation between several species, only one of which is doing the actual developing. It is," he stresses, "the unfolding of an entire ecosystem."

After a human baby is born, the collaborations between species grows even more complex. Like other mammals, human mothers make breast milk that contains lactose, fats, and complex sugar molecules called oligosaccharides. However, human breast milk contains more oligosaccharides than does the milk of other mammals—a lot more. As sugars are a great energy source, it makes sense that mothers would want to feed them to their rapidly growing newborns. But infants can't digest them. That realization, Yong notes, led scientists to investigate why humans bothered to make so many. As it turns out, one of the bacteria in the baby's gut, the Bifidobacterium *B. infantis*, can digest the complex sugars. When they do, they produce short-chain fatty acids as a by-product—and those short-chains nourish the baby's gut. So, the mother's milk nourishes the bacteria, bolstering their population. And the bacteria nourish the human baby's body.

Collaborations between microbes and humans aren't limited to early in life. The human gut contains more than four pounds of viruses, bacteria, and fungi; they help us digest food, influence our neurological states, and contribute to our immune systems—the very systems that thwart unwelcome microbes. Despite all that microbes do for humans, lots of folks resist considering them intrinsic to our selves. Not scientists, though. In *A Planet of Viruses*, the science writer Carl Zimmer points out that delineating a bright line between human beings and viruses isn't possible: "There is no us and them—just a gradually blending and shifting mix of DNA." We are all and always *we*.

The scholar Donna Haraway has long insisted as much, saying, "every being that matters is a congeries of its formative histories . . . even as any genome worth the salt to precipitate it is a convention of all the infectious events cobbled together into the provisional, permanently emerging things Westerners call individuals, but Melanesians, perhaps more presciently, call dividuals." We (in)dividuals are cobbled together, our genetic code comprised not just of human and microbial genes, but also of the many bits we share with honeybees and chimpanzees and even trees.

On the one hand, the overlap in our genomes with those of other beings, large and small, just makes sense: we very likely evolved from a common ancestor, and we all rely on just a few nucleotides to code for our every attribute. On the other hand, it's utterly mind-blowing: we very likely evolved from a common ancestor, and we all rely on just a few nucleotides to code for our every attribute.

As many gardeners do, I bought way too many seeds and then started far more plants than I need. Midwinter wishfulness leads me to overbuy, while pragmatism prompts me to start too many. I don't know how well the various seeds will germinate, so I plant more than I can use. That way, I'll have enough when some of them don't do well. I'm especially profligate with tomatoes because I grow heirlooms, which can be finicky, and I like to try a few new kinds each season. In March, I planted 144 tomato seeds in the seedling trays, far, far more than I have room to let grow into full-size plants. But the Barry's Crazy Cherry seeds didn't germinate at all, the Orange Bananas did terribly, and Mamie Brown's Pinks did just okay. On the other hand, the Radiator Charlie's Mortgage Lifters did wonderfully, as did the Yellow Brandywines. When the seedlings were large enough, I potted up and hardened off twice as many small plants as I would need. Now, my seedlings are all in the ground or in grow bags, and I still have plenty of leftover tomatoes and other plants.

This year, I'm giving many of them to the local AmeriCorps volunteer, who recently decided to start a garden at the school because the pandemic scrambled her plans for working with the children. After she takes what she can use, I bring the rest to the food pantry. The manager put a long conference table in the parking lot so folks could drop off plants at their convenience. When I arrive, dozens of pots containing tomatoes, beans, squashes, kales, chards, lettuces, and an array of herbs already cover the faux-wood surface. I add my offerings to this budding cornucopia.

THE FOOD PANTRY is busier than ever. With job layoffs, kids home from school, and empty store shelves, people are in need. Fortunately, during the first few weeks of the pandemic, several local families donated generously, anticipating that we'd see an increase in the number of clients. But we didn't fully anticipate how stark the situation would become. More people are coming, and the pantry is struggling to source enough food. Stores where the food pantry's manager normally bought items in bulk are imposing strict limits on how much customers can buy at a time. Where once we'd have bought two cases of canned corn, now we can buy just two cans. Already, the pantry has run through most of this year's food budget.

At first, we felt confident we'd have enough money to keep the pantry shelves full. We had that extra cash from local donors. Plus, back in March, FEMA announced funds would be available to defray almost all the increased costs at food pantries and other emergency facilities. But applying for FEMA funding turns out to be Sisyphean. The requirements change. The process changes. The due date changes. The amount each organization can apply for changes. Perhaps, someday, our application and FEMA's expectations will align for an instant, our grant will reach the right reader, it will be approved, and we will get reimbursed. Until then, I'm applying for other grants so the pantry can buy the many foods gardeners here can't grow.

I LIKE TO think of gardening as tending to life, giving the plants their best chance of thriving. But the obverse is equally true. Henry David Thoreau pointed out that gardening involves killing as well as nurturing, that the gardener makes "invidious distinctions with his hoe, levelling whole ranks of one species, and sedulously cultivating another." He's right: Gardening involves working hard to help members of some species survive in part by killing others to enhance the chances of the favored few. I pull plants I don't want, justify doing so by calling them weeds. I cull weak seedlings early on, cull some of the hardy ones later when thinning the carrots and beans and beets. After the harvest, Rob and I return the beds to blankness, prepare the soil to repeat this cycle the following spring.

Nor are plants the only beings whose fate I mediate. While I welcome moths and butterflies, ladybugs and bees, dragonflies and damsels, I concertedly kill Colorado potato beetles, Japanese beetles, and tomato hornworms. If they didn't cause so much damage, I'd admire the hornworms. In just two weeks, they grow from eggs into fat, four-inch-long pests that are practically invisible on a tomato plant because they're the exact color of its foliage, with whitish stripes that seem to mimic the spots where branching occurs on the plant. What enables that rapid growth is their voraciousness; they devour the foliage and fruit. A few years ago, when Kate, the same Kate who is part of our COVID task force, learned that hornworms are bioluminescent, she got black-light flashlights for all her gardener friends. Since then, instead of straining to spot the hornworms when they are huge and have done a lot of damage, I go out late at night and kill them while they are still young, no thicker than embroidery thread.

As much as the rabbits and weasels frustrate my gardening efforts, I don't kill rodents or small animals. Still, they often die in our yard because a garden is an unnatural place, one where their normal behavior can prove perilous. Each spring, we unearth nests of mice in the compost bins; warm, dark, with lots of nutrients in easy reach, the bins are mouse nirvana. But they can't stay, so I sink a shovel beneath each tangle of startled pink babies, lift them up and out on a layer of compost. At the tree line, I ease the shovel's contents to the ground. I doubt the mice will survive, as this small chance is all I feel able to offer. When a rabbit gets fatally ensnared in trellising, I cut away the confining net and carry the body to the edge of the yard, tuck it under some leaf litter.

Every year, birds fly into the windows of the house and greenhouse, thunking against the glass and falling down dazed. Most are up and off in a matter of moments, but for those who don't survive, I make more trips to the tree line, send them onward. Worse are the ones who are only *almost* dead. Last week, I found a female hairy woodpecker who couldn't move; already, pale green insects were troubling her eyes. Whispering promises that everything would be better soon, I picked her up and finished what her collision with the window set in motion.

IN HIS BOOK *Flight Ways*, Thom van Dooren offers a modification to the Buddhist proposition that "nothing ever exists entirely alone; everything is in relation to everything else." Instead, he suggests that "while we may all *ultimately* be connected to one another, the specificity and proximity of connections matters—*who we are bound up with and in what ways*. Life and death happen inside these relationships."

When I saw the dying woodpecker, I did feel bound to her, connected not only by empathy but also by guilt. I had transformed her flight way, placed a nearly invisible partition in her once-limitless space; if I hadn't, she might still be alive. Altering her world obliged me to her. I don't feel similarly bound to all woodpeckers everywhere, don't feel the same sense of obligation to them, even though I suspect I should. Admitting that feels shameful, unenlightened.

WHILE I FEEL obliged to not harm the deer who claim our yard as part of their range, I do not believe I owe them fine herbaceous meals. Topography makes installing an effective deer fence nearly impossible, so we've tried other disincentives to keep them out of the garden. Irish Spring soap, hair clippings, coyote urine, wind chimes, motion-sensitive strobe lights, even sweetly scented pest tasers have all worked for a day or a week or a season. Nothing's worked longer than that.

Last fall, a bulb catalog came in the mail, with a teaser on the front cover touting "deer proof" and "deer resistant" bulbs. Except for garlic, I'd never planted bulbs, but the idea of planting something so unpalatable the deer would avoid the garden tantalized. Thus began:

Operation Beautiful Deterrence

Step One: I looked up what else deer love and hate and discovered the day lilies lining our driveway were, in effect, a neon welcome sign advertising an all-you-can-eat buffet. We pulled them out and replaced them with daffodil and allium bulbs, both of which the catalog promised were "deer and rodent proof."

Step Two: We planted the garlic in one of the outermost beds, onions and cucumbers in the other one, as they're all described as "highly deer-resistant."

Step Three: In case the deer breached the perimeter, we added interior reinforcements. Among the vegetables rows we planted marigolds—extra-large blooms, long-lasting blooms, and double-blooms selected for maximal repulsion.

Step Four: Since deer find most herb scents offensive, I scattered pots of rosemary, dill, parsley, and lavender between the vegetable beds.

THE DAFFODILS AND allium did their job well, deterred deer from entering the garden from the driveway. But the daffodils were done blooming in early May, and the allium are beginning to fade now, meaning the garden periphery will be unprotected the rest of the season. This is a problem because the other plants are considerably less effective than their promoters promised. What should have been a rank, fetid plot where no deer would willingly dally is, instead, one where they trample the garlic on their way to the peas, bound through potatoes and marigolds in their eagerness to reach the beans, ignore the onions as they munch on nearby beet greens.

Truth be told, daffodils are not among my favorite flowers. Even so, I've ordered more. They have a canny strategy for enlisting humans in their dispersal. They don't need me to like them; they just need me to dislike them less than I dislike hungry deer, a vegetal version of "the enemy of my enemy is my friend."

IT'S NOT EVEN midway through June and already it's hot. Yesterday was almost 80 degrees. Today is expected to be hot, too, so I opened up the greenhouse extra early this morning to make sure the plants don't overheat. Inside it were a pair of panicky phoebes, fluttering and squeaking. I tried to shoo them toward the open door, but they stayed in a corner, their wings flapping furiously against a low, fixed pane. A few potted plants stood between them and the door, so I moved them aside. Once the path from corner to door was clear, I stepped well away, then watched them free themselves.

One of the birds hopped to a spot where a pot had been. Perhaps she registered the difference, for she soon bobbed to the door and flew out, landing in a nearby serviceberry. The other bird remained in the corner, crying out and fluttering. After several minutes, the brave bird flew back. She hopped into the greenhouse, stopped just inside the open door, called out to her friend, who continued to flap plaintively. The brave bird strutted toward her, got her attention, then hopped back toward the door. The other bird inched toward her, stopped halfway. Once more, the brave bird marched toward the other, then back to the open doorway. The scared bird hopped a few more steps, got a little closer to the door. They repeated the dance a third time. When they were close enough to feel the breeze coming in through the open door, or to sense some other something that let them know a way out was nigh, the pair flew up and out, landing in a lilac bush.

To me, it looked like the brave bird was taking care of the other one. Curious about how birds learn to do this, I searched online for stories of avian altruism. I couldn't find any, though I found plenty about "reciprocal altruism," instances of birds acting in ways that appear unselfish, but that actually benefit the not-technically-benevolent bird. Instances of reciprocal altruism seemed especially common among critters who are kin; helping one's sister or cousin increases the odds that some of the helper's DNA will make it into the next generation, even if the helper doesn't reproduce, since close relatives share many genes. Maybe that's what was happening with the phoebes. Maybe the brave bird only helped the other because they were relatives and she wanted to maximize the likelihood of her genes getting passed on.

Or, maybe, she really cared.

"CARE" COMES FROM Old Norse, from the word for "sorrow, anxiety, and grief." By 1400 CE, "care" in English had taken on the additional meanings of "to protect, to take care of." We take care of one another in the hope of avoiding or assuaging sorrows and grief.

Ironically, if we truly care, we inevitably experience sorrow and grief. Caring increases our permeability, causes us to let more in. That's no small thing, for we are already startlingly permeable—to viruses and other microbes, to ideas and beliefs, to emotions. And we don't just let things in, allow them to hang out for a bit, then send them on their merry way while we remain unchanged. No, what enters us alters us.

BY MIDMONTH, THE garlic and onions are tall, and all four kinds of potatoes, along with many varieties of beans, have popped through the soil. Two types of beets, of carrots, and of cucumbers, along with the shelling peas and snap peas and corn are growing apace. The heat-loving plants—the tomatoes, peppers, and melons—all lag, but even they are in their final containers or in the ground. And most of the herbs—mint, thyme, sage, rosemary, fennel, parsley, oregano, marjoram, basil, dill, and savory—are mature enough to use.

A decade ago, when I planted the oregano and marjoram in the herb bed, I didn't know they were members of the mint family, didn't know to segregate them or to prevent them from flowering if I wanted space for anything else. Every year, they claim more territory while I try to confine their quarters. As our battle continues, my side is modestly aided by the tenacity of the sages standing their ground; theirs is abetted by genetics, their fine roots spreading and producing suckers each spring.

I'VE FALLEN INTO war metaphors, operations and deterrence and enemies and perimeters and breaching, battles and quarters and territory. That's not how I want to regard the other denizens of this space, not how I want us to regard one another. And yet, I not only use the metaphors, I named the campaign and got a kick out of doing so. In retrospect, the ease with which I did it is unnerving.

I want a different script.

THINKING ABOUT THESE military metaphors has made me consider, yet again, the link epidemiologists draw between pandemics and agriculture. The changes hunter-gatherers made—

and continue to make—to their environments are more modest than those of agriculturalists. To be sure, hunter-gatherers clear land using fire, sow seeds for plants they desire, and overhunt many species. But the very nature of their food-getting incents them to work in concert with their surroundings so food will remain available.

Agriculture altered that dynamic. Agriculturalists also work with the environment, but somewhat differently. Early agriculturalists slowly altered the genomes of the plants they wanted to cultivate and the environment within which they grew—clearing more land, weeding out more undesirable plants, developing irrigation methods. When existing conditions didn't meet their desires, they modified the environment to make it more suitable. When their farming efforts worked, agriculturalists could imagine they were largely in charge, dwelling above, rather than amid, their surroundings. Focusing on that mental shift, from "amid" to "above," I sense a rather direct route leading from those first farms to empires maintained via warfare, and from those worlds to one inevitably roiled by pandemics.

A NEW WAY of having COVID-19 is emerging. People get sick, but not deathly so. Then they don't fully recover. In some cases, they can no longer concentrate, have brain fog. In others, ordinary exertion, like walking up a set of stairs, exhausts them. They call themselves "long haulers." Unlike the folks who end up on ventilators, many long haulers are young and were in good health beforehand. Immunologists don't know why this is happening, though they point out that many diseases have long-lasting aftereffects.

Kate refers to such symptoms by their medical name, "sequelae," the follow-ons to a disease. She stresses on our task force Zooms that folks who aren't worried about dying should still be cautious so they don't end up losing their sense of taste or smell, or becoming chronically exhausted, or develop whatever other sequelae doctors discover once the disease has been around awhile.

IN URGING PEOPLE to be careful so they can avoid sequelae, Kate is deliberately sidestepping any question of our obligation to others, strategically centering self-interest. But the pandemic has compelled me, and perhaps most people, to explore what van Dooren calls our "boundness" to others: Who am I bound up with? How am I bound? A first pass is easy; I am bound to Rob, to my relatives and my friends. Am I bound to my neighbors? My townspeople? My countrymen? If I am bound to the woodpeckers in our yard, then I am assuredly also bound to human neighbors. Does boundness stretch beyond the local? Can it? Should it? Must it?

I'm fascinated by van Dooren's assertion that "*who we are bound up with and in what ways*" is where the life and death matters happen—I want to understand the implications of that idea. At the same time, I have trouble with the word "bound," for it suggests the alternative exists—that we could be unbound, detached from one another, able to go solo. But we really can't. At the very least, we share the same air.

Early in my marriage, I used to think about that at night as I listened to Rob breathe. I was inhaling his exhale, drawing in not just the nitrogen and oxygen and carbon dioxide and argon he'd expelled, but the moisture and the trace of onion lingering on his breath, the pong of methane sharpening his saliva. And after my body took what it needed, some of his surplus nitrogen or oxygen or argon, perhaps, or a bit of carbon from the CO_2, I'd exhale the rest, return the unspent molecules to the air. Then it was Rob's turn to inhale my exhale. Young, nerdy, and in love, I thought we were extra intimately connected because we shared molecules.

But it's not just lovers who share air. We all inhabit this last remaining commons, breathing in and out, in and out, changing the atmosphere's local character with every respiration, altering what's available for everyone. In her book of poems *This Connection of Everyone with Lungs,* Juliana Spahr writes, "everyone with lungs breathes the space between the / hands and the space around the hands and the space of the / room and the space of the building that surrounds the room / and the space of the neighborhoods nearby and the space of / the cities and the space of the regions and the space of the / nations in and out."

We're built to be breathers; gravity makes it easy for our lungs to welcome in the space that enters and alters us, makes it easy to release that space. The coronavirus takes advantage of our biology, of the fact that we must breathe. As we breathe the space between, we risk making it toxic—unless we are careful, so very, very care-full.

HARD AS IT is to be cautious and attentive now, it was far more difficult when people didn't know about microbes, didn't understand the causes of disease. Two millennia ago, the physician Galen believed—as had Hippocrates before him—that illness occurred when someone's humors were out of balance and the person encountered miasma, the malodorous air near swamps and rotting matter. While neither of those ancient physicians knew about germs, the idea that people who aren't hale get sick when they encounter something gross in the air resonates with what doctors say today: those most likely to contract COVID-19 are people whose immune systems are weak and who breathe in air containing quite a bit of the coronavirus.

When Galen was a physician in the Roman Empire, a pandemic broke out. Lucius Verus and Marcus Aurelius Antoninus were co-emperors at the time, the last of the so-called Five Good Emperors. Under normal circumstances, emperors in ancient Rome claimed their thrones as a hereditary right, one passing from father to son. But some emperors had no sons. To get around that legacy-ending difficulty, an emperor could adopt a young man to succeed him, even though everyone knew the two were related neither by nature nor nurture. Both Lucius Verus and Marcus Aurelius were adoptees. In fact, five of the six emperors who ruled during the Pax Romana were adopted, which led Machiavelli to propose that their goodness offered insights into "how a good government is to be established; for while all the emperors who succeeded to the throne by birth, except Titus, were bad, all were good who succeeded by adoption."

The "pax" in Pax Romana is a relative term, for the emperors continued to wage war to maintain and attain territory. In 165 CE, Lucius Verus led troops on a crusade to take two cities in Mesopotamia, an important trade hub on the Tigris River. The Romans won that round of the centuries-long conflict and returned home feeling triumphant, but the victory was pyrrhic. During the battle, Roman troops destroyed a temple dedicated to Apollo, and in punishment (so the soldiers assumed) Apollo sent a disease that soon spread through their legions. The new illness decimated the Roman army. Those who didn't succumb dispersed the disease, carrying the pathogen for the Antonine Plague wherever they went. Rome was hit especially hard, with as many as two thousand people dying each day.

Galen wrote that those who became ill suffered sore throats, fever, thirstiness, vomiting, and bloody stool. Pustular rashes covered their bodies. Two years into the Antonine Plague outbreak, the co-emperors summoned Galen to come care for them at their winter quarters. But the region became a viral hot spot, and "the emperors fled immediately to Rome with a small force of men." Verus died en route. Outbreaks continued for more than a decade, abated over the following decade, then returned. Five to ten million people died, around 10 percent of the population of the Roman Empire.

Those who survived had a re-ordered sense of their place in the world. A renewed attention to magic and a broader embrace of Christianity followed the outbreak. For people then, as for us, time was "both structured by the epidemic . . . and unstructured by its continuity, by the uncertainty of its end."

WHAT WILL THE reordered world look like for us? What will "normal" be in the wake of the pandemic? Already, many Americans are growing skeptical about science, eager to eschew the emergency measures epidemiology dictates. Will that loss of confidence be countered by a greater faith in something else, something spiritual or mystical, as happened after the Antonine Plague? Or will those doubts get forgotten if scientists are able to create a vaccine?

YESTERDAY, JUNE 28, the world marked two terrible pandemic milestones. The number of known cases crossed ten million and the number of known deaths crossed half a million. Even so, our bubble decided to stick to our plan to meet in person. We stayed outside in Tom and Susan's yard, sitting far apart. I think we all needed to reassure ourselves that we can accommodate the virus without succumbing to it or to loneliness. Being together was fantastic, though everyone seemed *extra*. Maybe that was just my perception, unaccustomed to seeing anyone but Rob in 3D after all this time on Zoom. Or maybe three months with limited human contact has atrophied my social senses. Or maybe we really were extra; maybe we're all so out of practice being social that we're unconsciously performing our former selves.

THE HAWTHORN IS finally in flower and is attracting every pollinator not currently seduced by something purple. A thick, whirring cloud coalesces each morning in and around the tree's low canopy. Hundreds of individual insects buzz and hum, each intent on its own efforts, and the accumulated clamor swells and fades, swells and fades, like a single being breathing.

JULY

⟡ ⟡

THE STEWARTIA IS flowering, its showy white petals
broadly open, pale yellow pistils exposed. Most of the other
trees are done flowering; many have moved on to fruit.

COVID-19 CASES WORLDWIDE have reached almost
eleven million, with more than five hundred thousand deaths.
The US has nearly 2.8 million cases and over 130,000 deaths.
Nationally, the virus is spiraling out of control; there were
more than fifty thousand new cases overnight, the record for
a single day and the fifth record for a single day in the last two
weeks. To tame this rampant spread, Dr. Fauci is urging Americans to stay home over the Fourth of July.

In our corner of Maine, the Fourth of July is when most
of the summer people return. This year, many came in the
spring—when lockdowns began in their other home states.
Our COVID-19 task force prepared paper fliers and website

pages full of information to help the newly arrived get through self-quarantines: lists of places that deliver food, alcohol, and medicine, places where one can get tested, restaurants doing takeout—basically, everything we could think of to help make two weeks of isolating easier. We gave paper copies to folks who manage short-term rentals so they could share the lists with visitors and circulated the information in the post offices and on several websites. To our surprise, some people were offended. They thought we were being prejudiced, that we were suggesting new arrivals would make people in Saint George sick.

ON JULY 6, the Trump administration announces that the president sent a letter to the United Nations alerting them of the United States' intention to withdraw from the World Health Organization because the WHO is capitulating to pressure from China "to mislead the world" about the new coronavirus. I doubt that's true, not only because there's little evidence to support his claim, but also because news reports reached the West today about a herdsman in Inner Mongolia who has bubonic plague. I have a hard time imagining the WHO would help China "mislead the world" about the pandemic but would allow the news to get out that someone has *the* plague, the one that caused millions of people to die during the Black Death in medieval Europe.

I'm pretty sure a bubonic plague outbreak atop a COVID-19 pandemic is more than the world can handle. It's more than I can handle. And yet, I can't look away. Learning about other pandemics began as a way to gain perspective, to see our situation within a larger context. Now, whenever a news story connects COVID-19 to some other pandemic, I want to know more about the other outbreak. I'm still looking for parallels. But I'm also looking for hope, for accounts of the lengths to which good leaders and ordinary citizens went to care for one another. Sometimes, hope comes simply from knowing we humans still exist, that the world has rebounded from crises far worse than we now face.

So I began to doomscroll the bubonic plague, which is how I found out the Black Death had a precedent, that *another* round of bubonic plague had roiled the world centuries earlier. When it began, the Roman Empire was already in disarray. A century-long series of battles with neighbors had gone poorly, and the western portion of the Roman Empire had been lost. What remained were the eastern Empire and a few outposts. The capital had relocated to Constantinople, and a plague outbreak that began in Egypt in 541 CE reached Constantinople the following year. Justinian I was Emperor at the time, so this pandemic became known as the Justinian Plague.

Like Marcus Aurelius Antoninus and Lucius Vero, Justinian wasn't a direct descendent of an emperor; he was the nephew of one. When Justinian succeeded his uncle, he had big aspirations: he wanted to bring the Roman Empire back to its former size and power. And he did accomplish quite a bit. In a *New Yorker* essay last April about pandemics and how they help shape history, Elizabeth Kolbert pointed out that Justinian I "codified Roman law, made peace with the Persians, overhauled the Eastern Empire's fiscal administration, and built the Hagia Sophia." But he did not manage to rebuild the Roman Empire; to the contrary, he was the last Roman emperor.

In his book *Justinian's Flea: The First Great Plague and the End of the Roman Empire*, William Rosen argues that while human folly and ordinary foes set the Roman Empire on its downward trajectory, the late, decisive blow was delivered not by Goths or Vandals, but by the bacterium *Yersinia pestis*, which causes bubonic plague. *Y. pestis* is typically carried by a specific flea, *Xenopsylla cheopsis*, that likes to live in the gut of black rats. These rats often lived aboard ships that traveled the Nile and others that crisscrossed the Mediterranean and Aegean Seas.

Black rats were common on ships, but bubonic plague was normally confined to East Africa. Its spread was constrained by the narrow temperature ranges within which the bacterium and the flea could each do their thing. *X. cheopsis* is only active in a small temperature range, 59–68 degrees. And *Y. pestis* doesn't reproduce much inside the flea if the ambient temperature is over 75 degrees. So as ships traveling northward on the Nile neared Alexandria, the fleas and bacteria would overheat; the bacteria wouldn't reproduce, the fleas wouldn't eat. To be sure, plenty of rats carrying infected fleas reached the docks in Constantinople under ordinary circumstances, but not enough to trigger a crisis.

Then, during the late 530s, a dust-veil cloaked the upper atmosphere. Because of the dust, less sunlight reached earth; the planet grew enough cooler that this era is known as the Late Antique Little Ice Age. The *Y. pestis* in the fleas could continue reproducing, and the fleas remained active. In 542 CE, rather than a few rats carrying a few infected fleas into

Constantinople, many heavily infested rats arrived. Fleas carrying the plague bacteria usually bite rats or other rodents. But as *Y. pestis* continued to reproduce in the gut of its flea host, the bacterial populations rose so much that they needed to find many new hosts. The crafty bacteria created obstructions in the fleas' digestive systems that prevented them from absorbing nutrients from the blood they ate. Starving, the fleas grew desperate and bit like crazy, nipping any available source of blood—including humans. The fleas' saliva contained bacteria, which entered the new hosts.

At first, people who'd been bitten felt like they had a flu, had fevers and headaches, maybe chills and general weakness. Then the victims developed black lumps—buboes—in their groins or armpits as the rapidly reproducing bacteria built up in their lymph nodes. Eventually, the lymph nodes burst, oozing blood and pus. About 80 percent of those who became ill died. In Constantinople alone, as many as five thousand people were dying each day at the height of the outbreak. Overwhelmed hospitals served more as sites to house the dying than as places offering cures. Justinian paid for the dead to be buried, but so many died so quickly that the streets filled with bodies. Soon, the plague jumped the city walls; as *Y. pestis* continued their travels, disease ravaged broad swaths of the world.

Procopius, a historian in that era, compared Justinian to the plague, calling him "a second pestilence sent from heaven." And while Justinian certainly had many strengths as a leader, his weaknesses did make him especially ill-suited to lead during a pandemic. Those frailties almost certainly made the outbreak and its repercussions far worse than they would have been under a wiser leader. Justinian was a man of "enormous ego . . . distinctly wanting in respect to his predecessors." And while he wanted to reunite a geographic empire, he had little interest in bringing actual people together. Instead, he preferred playing them off one another for his own benefit, which was easy to do in Constantinople, where the two main political factions specialized in generating foment. Neither confined itself to strongly worded op-eds; to the contrary, "in Constantinople, the road that led from formal debate to sloganeering to abusing officials to street violence was a short one." Even before he was emperor, "Justinian recognized the factions were a powerful political force that he could harness to his own ambition."

Justinian's voracious egotism was not tempered by his success; another chronicler of his era wrote that "Justinian was insatiable in the acquisition of wealth, and . . . excessively covetous of the property of others." His aides understood Justinian's need to appear peerless: "Above all, the emperor's men possessed ambition enough to be successful, but enough loyalty to value their emperor's success above their own." Maintaining "a cosmic sense of his own destiny," Justinian displayed the "ill-disciplined energy of all insomniacs as he paced the palace corridors at night." He rarely ventured far from home: "He left his capital seldom, if at all, except to visit nearby vacation palaces," though he did have "a mania for attaching his chosen name to geographical and political enterprises without number."

During the initial plague outbreak, between 20 and 40 percent of the population of Constantinople perished. Justinian himself became ill, and rumors spread of his death. In 455 CE, he wishfully declared the plague over. His desires notwithstanding, localized outbreaks continued for the next two hundred years, including flare-ups in Constantinople in 558, 573, and 586 CE. The plague reached as far north as Ireland and east to Asia Minor; it killed between twenty-five and fifty million people, one-seventh of the world's population. Cities shrank, towns disappeared. Humans returned, mostly, to rural living.

A LEADER WITH an enormous ego and an abiding sense of his own "cosmic" destiny, one who demanded total loyalty, who was insatiably covetous. A leader who pitted people against one another, used their fractiousness to fuel his own desires. An insomniac who fretfully paced at night, anxious about his own status. A leader who simply asserted a pandemic was over. This isn't the sort of leader suited to guiding people during a dire public health crisis.

And yet, once again, this is the sort of leader many of us have.

TWO DAYS AFTER the news about the Chinese herdsman reached the West, the press reported that Brazil's President Bolsonaro tested positive for the coronavirus. The virus is widespread in Brazil, but Bolsonaro consistently downplays its seriousness. Now that he's acknowledging he has COVID-19, I'm even more worried for Brazil's people. What I most fear is the virus spreading into the rainforest and destroying the remaining hunter-gatherer populations there, like the Pirahã, who live on a tributary of the Amazon River. If people without access to hospitals and ventilators contract the virus, can they survive?

Or will they vanish, taking their cultures and languages and ways of life with them?

My interest in the Pirahã was sparked a dozen years ago when I learned about their unusual language, also called Pirahã. It's extremely compact, with only eleven speech sounds in the men's language and ten in the women's. The women's version has fewer speech sounds than any other language in the world, and one of those sounds is extremely unusual, found in only half a dozen languages. The content of the language is also quite constrained, with few words for denoting what we often think of as fundamental ideas, including colors, numbers, and kin relationships. Pirahã has words to distinguish relative lightness or darkness, but not colors or hues. And without words for numbers or a counting system, Pirahã has few ways to express quantities, sizes, ages, and time intervals. It has just one word for "parent," which applies to mothers and fathers, and no words for kin beyond parents and siblings, making their kinship system one of the simplest in any documented language.

Most intriguingly, at least if you love language as much as I do, Pirahã appears to lack recursion, the method for adding detail to a sentence by embedding phrases inside linguistically similar phrases, like verbal Matryoshka nesting dolls. If I want to add greater detail to the sentence "Margot grows plants," I can add the noun phrase "she and Rob can eat" to modify "plants." Saying "Margot grows plants she and Rob can eat" is both more concise and informative than saying "Margot grows plants. Margot can eat plants. Rob can eat plants." Using recursion connects related pieces of information while compressing sentence length.

Recursion might just sound like a nerdy bit of grammar, but before linguists knew about Pirahã, they considered it a general property of language *because every other known language has recursion*. Its prevalence suggests recursion provides a way to express a universal thinking pattern. But if Pirahã doesn't have it, that could mean its native speakers make sense of the world in a fundamentally different way than does everyone else. And if that's true, then why? And how?

Of course I wonder what a lack of recursion could mean about Pirahã speakers. But I also wonder about other possibilities their unusual language creates: If they aren't trying to decide exactly what shade of blue something is, or whether someone is a second cousin or a first cousin once removed, what apprehensions might they be having instead? Does a mind behold colors differently if it doesn't make verbal distinctions? Do people with few words for kinship view everyone beyond their immediate family as comparably close relations or as equally distant? Does the lack of a counting system make them unconcerned about quantities? Relative ages? Time's passage?

If the Pirahã succumb to the coronavirus, what unique ideas or beliefs might vanish?

ONE OF MY brothers and I are on a communication hiatus; every time we talk or email, we fight. He goads me, and I can't not take the bait. Lately, he's been saying the pandemic is overhyped and that, come year's end, we'll learn that no more people died than in an average year. I insist he's wrong, but can't help adding that even if he's right, dying of COVID-19 and dying gently in one's sleep are hardly equivalent for the dying person or the folks they love. He reminds me that most of the deaths have been among people over seventy-five, implying their ages mitigate the tragedy. I remind him his mother is over seventy-five. After I accused him of callousness and he called me a snowflake, we stopped talking.

Not talking is less stressful than talking, but I hate having come to this impasse. Over the years, we've disagreed about plenty of things, but we never lost access to a common language. Now ordinary nouns—words like "risk," "loss," "danger," "significance"—no longer mean the same thing to us both. Before we stopped bickering, we resorted to parsing each other's emails, critiquing word choice. Small-hearted as that sounds (because it was), it points to the crux of our problem: We lack a shared language. Without one, we can talk at, over, or past each other—but not with.

WE'VE BEEN FOGGED since the ninth, "socked in," as folks say here. Four days and counting of being mired in the kind of dense, blank fog more common to early June. The spruces edging the yard look like shadows on a scrim, their bows gray where the fog's thickest, green where it thins. My world grows smaller while the one beyond disappears entirely. But even with fog obscuring the larger world, I can't ignore it. My body is stuck in one place, but my mind refuses to stay put.

FORTUNATELY, THE GARDEN keeps me fully grounded for some stretch of each day. Right now, the plants are starting to give back in earnest, and I have plenty of harvesting to do. The strawberries are plump and red and sweeter than I'd expected, given the recent lack of sunshine. I pick all that are ready each day. The green beans, salad greens, kale, and herbs are coming on strong. As are the garlic scapes—my new favorite. I've long admired how they look, standing tall until their tips thicken and get light, almost white, where the bulbils grow. That tip is technically a flower. Once it fattens, the scapes curl, make a loop or two. Somehow, I didn't know to eat the scapes before. But this year, as soon as the scapes began to curl, I started harvesting them, cutting them just a few inches above the soil line. We are eating them both raw and grilled, and I made a batch of especially delicious pesto using scapes in place of half the basil.

Quite a few plants have more than one edible part. I once went foraging with a guy who said every part of milkweed can be eaten, provided you eat each at the right time of year. Though I believe him, I leave the milkweed for the butterflies, limit myself to plants I'm more confident consuming. From our garden, we can eat both beet greens and beet roots, squash blossoms and squashes. Garlic scapes seem extra special, though, because harvesting them is not simply possible, it's a good idea: Doing so benefits the bulb. Because the plant is being deprived of the chance to flower, it directs all the energy that would have gone into flowering down into the bulb, making it bigger.

BETWEEN GETTING OLDER and my never-ending horsetail battle (another war metaphor, damn), I don't enjoy weeding as much as I used to. For years, I took pleasure in creating temporarily neat rows. Now, I find most weeding tedious. But today, I've been pulling vetch, which is so easy and satisfying that I don't mind at all.

As weeds go, vetch is awesome. It's pretty, easy to spot, and doesn't have barbs or other sharp bits. Granted, its roots are really rhizomes, so I rarely remove all the thready supports, but there's a pleasure in pulling out yard-long strands in one go. Vetch took hold in the bed where I tried to grow wheat and in one where I grew black garbanzo beans years ago; the young bean plants and young vetch look similar enough that the weed got a solid start before I could tell them apart. It crisscrosses the groundcover on the outcropping where the azalea is. And if I don't pay attention to it soon enough, it cloaks the ferns out front.

While I consider vetch a weed, humans viewed it as food for thousands of years. Learning that led me to think about how arbitrary the category "weed" can be. A weed, according to the *Merriam-Webster Dictionary*, is "a plant that is not valued where it is growing and is usually of vigorous growth." Weeds are weeds not by virtue of their genes or intrinsic qualities, but by virtue of how they're regarded. So if I value vetch, it will cease to be a weed, will be elevated to non-weedy glory. I—we—can will something out of categorical humbleness simply by loving it.

ALONG WITH PEAS and lentils, vetch was an important source of protein for early agriculturalists, one of the foods that helped humans transition from a nomadic to a sedentary lifestyle. Early farmers didn't know these legumes were an excellent source of protein, but they knew they were somehow beneficial. By 2000 BCE, domesticated peas were grown as far west as Portugal, east to the Indus Valley, and north to Denmark. European settlers who came to the Americas brought peas to the New World. Likewise, ancient farmers didn't know that legumes could fix nitrogen, but they knew they did something that improved soil quality; Xenophon, writing in the fourth century BCE, pointed out that they revitalized exhausted soil.

Humans still eat peas and lentils, but at some point, most stopped eating vetch, maybe because not all vetches are safe to eat. Some contain chemicals that act as neurotoxins and are debilitating when consumed in large quantities. Now, when grown intentionally, vetches are primarily cover crops.

I grow vetch inadvertently, but I grow garden peas deliberately and with great delight. This year's varieties are Green Arrow and Sutton's Harbinger, both shelling peas originally from England; Golden Snow Peas, originally from India; Sugar Ann, an early ripening sugar snap pea; and Beauregarde, a brand new purple snow pea from the vegetable company Row 7. Sutton's Harbinger vines are quite short, so they can be grown in a container with a small trellis. I started a large container of them in the greenhouse back in March and moved it outside in early May. We didn't get a lot of peas from that single pot—but we got them in mid-June, nearly a month before any of the other peas were ripe.

Now, mid-July, we have a pea bonanza that will last several weeks. The golden pea pods are ready, and the Green Arrow shelling peas and Sugar Ann snaps are starting to come on. I'm not sure when the Beauregardes will be ready; they look to be several weeks behind the others. The goldens grow tallest of all our peas, with vines that stretch more than six feet high. Some of the plants still have beautiful, purply flowers, but most of the blooms have given way to bright lemon-yellow pods. Like the more common green version, golden pea pods are best eaten while they're still flat, before the peas themselves mature. I eat lots of them straight from the vine. The ones that make it to the kitchen usually end up in salads, as they are so delicate that steaming them is unnecessary.

Since the Sugar Ann and Green Arrow pea pods are starting to feel fat and full, I check the vines each morning so I can pick the pods at their peak. If I miss it, and the pods begin to lose their faint sheen and start to roughen, the peas themselves will begin converting sugars into starch. They'll taste less sweet. Plus, if I'm diligent about picking the peas at peak ripeness, and if we don't get a string of too-hot days, the plants will continue to flower and fruit well into August. After gathering the readiest, which today are almost all Green Arrows, I set the bowl on the kitchen counter and cover it with a dish towel, so the pods and tendrils don't tempt the cats. I'll shell them right before dinner.

Whether prepping enough for a meal or for a batch to freeze, shelling peas is one of my favorite summer tasks. It doesn't feel like work; it's more like meditation. I love the repetition of snapping one end of the pod, splitting it open along the stringed seam, casually inspecting the peas as I thumb each one away from the tiny stalk connecting it to the pod. Love the plink-thunk sound they make tumbling into the bowl, how the sound changes, grows more muffled, as they accumulate. On especially pea-replete days, Rob helps shell. Even with us both standing there, the cats try to climb up onto the counter, unable to resist the allure of the pods. Every few minutes, Rob tosses an emptied pod to the floor to distract them from the bounty before us.

BEAUREGARDE PEAS HAVE only been on the market for a year, so I don't yet know what to expect of them. They were developed by Michael Mazourek, a plant breeder who worked in collaboration with the chef Dan Barber. They wanted to create a purple pea that held its color when cooked, that wasn't chewy or stringy, and that was just as sweet and tender as a great green pea. I don't know about the flavor or texture yet, but they achieved the color goal: the pods are an intense royal purple with chartreuse tips at the stem ends.

To develop Beauregarde, Mazourek crossed purple and green peas. In each generation, he kept the peas that had more of the qualities he desired, used them to make new sets of crosses. Achieving both a bold purple hue and a sweet pea flavor was tricky, as the same chemical that creates purple often makes plants bitter. But Mazourek managed to develop peas with all the desired traits, and with seeds that would consistently develop into plants with those traits. His general method was old-school, using the same plant-crossing process farmers have used for thousands of years. But he also bene-fitted from contemporary technology. Before making new crosses, he sent plant material from the potential parents to a lab to get their genomes sequenced. The more he knew about each potential parent, the more efficient he could be in mak-ing the crosses.

THOUGH FARMERS HAVE crossbred plant lines for millen-nia, they've only recently learned how the traits of one genera-tion reach the next. Natural philosophers who speculated about such matters were equally hard-pressed to explain the process—though they offered some intriguing theories.

Until the middle of the nineteenth century, the prevailing view was that an embryo was "preformed," that a perfect minia-ture entity was housed in either a sperm cell or an egg. Preform-ists thought the small being had existed since creation and was waiting for fertilization to provide the spark of life. The Greek philosopher Pythagoras believed the proto-babies were found in sperm cells and eggs simply supplied material to nourish the preformed being. In the 1600s, the British physician William Harvey challenged that view, not by proposing a new under-standing of how traits are inherited, but by reversing the roles of egg and sperm, arguing that the egg was home to the preformed being, and the sperm enlivened it.

By the nineteenth century, many botanists thought the preformists were wrong, but they lacked an alternative theory. Gregor Mendel, an Augustinian monk, was among those who set out to discover how traits are passed from one generation to the next. In his search for the mechanism, he spent eight years crossbreeding peas and comparing the traits of the offspring to those of their parents.

Starting with purebred lines, Mendel created hybrids and recorded how often specific traits appeared in subsequent generations. From the work of others who studied hybrids, he knew the peas in his first harvest would all look alike. He dubbed the characteristics that appeared in the first generation of hybrids "dominant," those that didn't "recessive." Moreover, thanks to having grown up on a farm, he knew the source for the recessive traits was still there, somewhere, because recessive traits could—and often did—show up in future generations of plants or animals. Sure enough, in the next generation of peas, the offspring of the first hybrids, the recessive traits reappeared. To Mendel's amazement, they showed up in a predictable ratio: three-quarters of the peas had the dominant trait, while one-quarter had the recessive trait.

After that, things got more complicated. The offspring of the second generation of hybrids with the recessive trait all looked like the parent. Not so for the offspring of the second generation hybrids with the dominant trait. For one-third of them, all the offspring had the dominant trait. For the other two-thirds, the offspring displayed the dominant traits three out of four times. Studying all the relevant traits, doing so in dozens of different configurations, Mendel found these ratios again and again. The first generation looked alike. The second had a 3:1 ratio of dominant to recessive appearances. And in the third generation, among the dominant-looking plants, "two-thirds of the plants have hybrid-character, while one-third remains constant with the dominant character," and the recessive plants all continued to show the recessive trait.

Mendel kept going, eventually growing more than ten thousand pea plants as part of his experiment. But the laws he sought, the discovery that made him famous and inaugurated the study of genetics, are found in these ratios. Without knowing there was such a thing as a gene, Mendel was able to deduce that some internal kernel carried information about parental traits to subsequent generations, where it was intermingled in a predictable manner. For sexually reproducing species, neither the egg alone nor the sperm alone determined the traits of the next generation; instead, both contributed to it in some as-yet-unknown, but orderly fashion.

MENDEL'S DISCOVERIES WERE lost for several decades, then resurfaced at the beginning of the twentieth century. Scientists of that era discovered that chromosomes are comprised of the information packets Mendel insisted had to exist; they called the packets "genes," the area of inquiry "genetics." Fast forward barely more than a century: Now, we know that both DNA and RNA carry genetic information. We understand how genes code information and pass it on, as well as how mutations occur. We have mapped the whole human genome and those of many other animals and even more plants.

And in Shanghai in January 2020, a virologist named Zhang Yongzhen led a team mapping the genome for a previously unknown virus that was making people ill in Wuhan, China. Sensing the urgency of the situation, the team worked nonstop for two days and nights, completing the first genetic map of SARS-CoV-2 in less than forty hours. Their genome map, along with others created since, are now helping scientists as they work to develop antiviral treatments and vaccines that will work against COVID-19.

OVER THE LAST few weeks, tens of thousands of people in the US, UK, Canada, Europe, and New Zealand received packets of seeds in the mail that they didn't order, my mother among them. Some of the packages were stamped "China Post," others had character-based writing on the packages or return addresses from China, prompting news outlets to dub them "Chinese Mystery Seeds."

When the seeds began arriving in the United States, regional agricultural extension services were flooded with anxious calls. At the outset, the local agencies offered conflicting advice, variously telling people to toss the seeds or to cook them at 200 degrees or to bring them to a local facility or to send them to the USDA. My mother thought the package she received looked odd and threw it away, unaware of the commotion the seeds were causing elsewhere.

Soon the USDA weighed in. They urged people to wear gloves if they handled the packages or seeds. Some officials worried the seeds were part of a bioterrorism campaign; they considered the possibilities that a harmful invasive species was being introduced, or that the seeds were coated with banned pesticides that would enter the soil and water. Others theorized the seeds were American in origin, part of a "'deep state' strategy to control our gardens . . . or a Chinese cure for COVID-19 [being] suppressed by Big Pharma." The one piece of advice all officials agreed on was the seeds should not, under any circumstances, be planted. Yet thousands of people acknowledged planting unfamiliar seeds from an unknown source and, incredibly, quite a few people reported eating them.

In an ever more porous world, it's our own nature that most imperils us.

MY NEPHEW ALEX and I have been Zooming in French on Fridays for the last month or so. He just finished seventh grade and has been in a French immersion program since he started school. I took a few years of French classes forever ago. I can read French well enough to get by in a restaurant or museum, but I can't understand spoken French very well. So when school ended for Alex in June, I cajoled him into being my chat-partner. He's patient for a twelve-year-old and speaks slowly so I can hear each word. Even so, our conversations are stilted, as our vocabularies overlap only in the most rudimentary areas.

Yesterday, he tried to explain Fortnite to me. I suspect it would have been confusing had he been speaking English, but in French, a language in which I don't know the words for "pickax" or "assault rifle" or "potion," it was impossible. That may be why I got distracted by a mama deer and two fawns who stepped out of the woods and onto the edge of our lawn. The doe stopped, and the babies bumped her gently, waiting as she surveyed the stretch of grass between them and the trees on the other side of the yard. Then all three minced across, picking their way along a narrow band of grass studded with stones. Though small and tentative, the fawns looked healthy, their umber pelts smattered with white dots. The doe, on the other hand, looked terrible. She was gaunt, as if she hadn't regained any weight after giving birth, and her fur looked mangy and tick-pocked.

I interrupted Alex to tell him what I was seeing. I have no idea what the words are for "deer tick" or "mangy" or "emaciated" in French. So I said the doe was *mince, trop mince*, and asked Alex if he knew the word for "insect." Then, giving up on French, I told him in English about the deer family and about *Operation Beautiful Deterrence*, my plan to keep deer out of the garden. Seeing this undernourished doe, I added, was making me feel guilty about how hard I'd worked to deprive her of food. Alex was noncommittal, unsure (I think) whether I was serious.

This morning, I went out to check the garden. The doe— or some other deer—had come in the night. The bean plants and cucumbers had all been neatly topped, every blossom eaten.

AUGUST

॰॰॰

T HE PERSON I most want to see, but can't, is my mom. She lives alone now, and in the Before Times, I visited her a couple times a month. The last time I saw her was March 12, which feels like years ago. My sister, who lives about forty miles from her, has visited her a few times this summer. They sit outside, far apart. But my mom lives two hundred miles from me and Rob, and I just can't fathom stopping at a highway rest area for gas, much less using the restroom at one. My youngest brother got our mom set up with Zoom, but she doesn't like it, especially if more than one or two other people are on a call. A friend suggested an Echo Show, a little video screen that can be programmed to use voice commands. Rob was able to set it up for her remotely, so she can just tell it "call Margot," and it will. While it's a poor substitute for true human contact, it's been a boon. Now, I can see her, albeit in miniature on my cell phone screen.

NEARLY EIGHTEEN MILLION COVID-19 cases have been reported, 4.7 million of them in the US. I cannot wrap my head around the fact that more than a quarter of all cases are here, in one of the world's richest nations. No, that's not quite accurate; if I do sit with this fact, really let myself absorb it, I get racked with despair.

THE METEOROLOGIST ON the local NPR affiliate keeps describing the weather as "unseasonably warm." But it's not warm, unseasonably or otherwise; it's hot. Last month was one of the hottest Julys on record in Maine. The temperature exceeded 90 degrees five days and was in the 80s on fifteen others. So far, August isn't any cooler.

The heat is emboldening the deer. I don't think they would bother eating rough cucumber leaves if they had plenty of fresh water available in more palatable forms. And the garden is already strained by the high temperatures themselves. The granite blocks that help so much at the beginning and end of the season by retaining heat are drying out the soil faster than I can keep the plants watered. The hot stretch has sapped the pea plants' vigor; we won't have a long harvest this year. And the tomatoes aren't ripening, something that's never happened before. A Google search reveals the heat is to blame for that, too. They don't ripen when it's consistently over 85 degrees, so I spend half the day today trimming them back and pinching off suckers in hopes an aggressive pruning would improve air circulation and they'd feel less overheated. Then I give them all an extra dose of fertilizer, fish emulsion diluted with cool water.

I'm overheated, too, and the stench of rank foliage and rotten fish is nauseating. It'll dissipate soon, I remind myself, and try to feel grateful that I'm safe outside and that I can spend so much time taking care of plants. The news is full of accounts of people sweltering inside because being hot and indoors is less risky than going to crowded playgrounds or parks or beaches.

THIS ODD HOT stretch is almost certainly related to general climate disruption. I haven't seen any accounts suggesting climate change is linked to the current pandemic, but I wonder. Several earlier pandemics were made possible—or made worse—by small climactic changes. Like the Justinian Plague that began in 542 CE, the Black Death of the medieval era was also a bubonic plague outbreak precipitated by a change in the global climate.

Early in the thirteenth century, Genghis Khan expanded the Mongol Empire into the largest empire that had, then, ever been. The expansion trajectories Khan and his successors pursued made not only military and political sense, but also climate sense. The Mongols were pastoralists who needed to graze their horses, but much of their core territory was growing colder, and the winters were lasting longer, because glaciers in Greenland and pack ice in the North Atlantic were expanding and moving south. Then, in 1257 CE, a massive volcanic eruption in Indonesia spewed ash and aerosols into the atmosphere, decreasing the amount of sunlight that could reach the earth. Three smaller volcanic eruptions occurred soon after, in 1268, 1275, and 1284, compounding the effects of the initial explosion. The combination of migrating ice pack and volcanic residue in the atmosphere contributed to a period of cooling known as the Little Ice Age.

The Mongols' historic territory was growing unpleasantly colder, but parts of the Central Asian steppes that had been desert were getting more precipitation and were becoming lush enough to accommodate grazing animals. Mongol warriors and their horses began to dwell there. Unfortunately, *Y. pestis*, the bacterium that causes bubonic plague, was already enzootic to that region, living in wild rodents. The slightly cooler temperature range of the Little Ice Age benefitted both *Y. pestis*, which could reproduce for a longer period, and their flea hosts, who were able to remain active longer. The level of disease carried by the rodents rose—much as it had for the shipboard rats that triggered the Justinian Plague. The fleas and bacteria ran out of their usual hosts, so they jumped to new ones, people among them. By the 1340s, Mongol warriors were succumbing to bubonic plague.

Due to the tremendous expansion of Mongol territory, the Silk Road network was then entirely under their control, which had mixed consequences for travelers' safety. On the one hand, risk of attacks by Mongol rivals was substantially reduced, so traders were more comfortable moving between China and Europe, which reinvigorated commerce. On the other hand, the influx of traders brought more people and animals into contact with the plague. Even traders who were not themselves plague victims were often its couriers, unknowingly carrying *Y. pestis* with them, lodged in the bodies of the rats in their caravans. By the summer of 1347, plague-bearing rats reached the Black Sea. From there, ships carried them to Constantinople and Messina and Marseille. Plague-infected people and rats travelled from those ports by both land and sea, bringing the disease to northern Africa, the Mediterranean, Europe. By 1348, it reached England, then Wales, then Denmark, Sweden, Russia, and Greenland.

To HALT THE pandemic's spread, the port authority in the Venetian-controlled port of Ragusa ordered ships coming from plague-infected locales to isolate for thirty days (a *trentina* in Italian). As it became clear that isolating ships did curb the spread of the plague, other ports introduced similar strictures. Over time, the length of the isolation period was increased to forty days, a *quarantina*. Venetians and others instituted additional public health measures much like those being urged today, including isolating the ill at home or in special hospital units and limiting people's movement in public spaces.

MAINE'S FIRST LOCKDOWN order, announced 144 days ago, was followed by several more, the last of which expired on June 11. However, we remain in a "State of Civil Emergency," and I remain homebound, halfway through my fourth consecutive *quarantina*. How different might the disease trajectory have been if the US and other hard-hit nations had implemented robust quarantines back in March, as New Zealand did? Could we have curbed the spread of COVID-19 enough to allow most people to move freely and confidently now? Could I safely leave the yard?

SOON AFTER THE Black Death reached Florence, the poet Boccaccio began writing *The Decameron*, the fictional stories of ten people who took refuge in a villa high on a hill beyond the city limits, where they hoped to escape the plague. Boccaccio observed that people reacted to the plague in four distinct ways. Some Florentines decided "living moderately and being abstemious would really help them to resist the disease," diverting themselves by "playing music and whatever other amusements they could devise." Others took a counter tack, believed that "the surest medicine for such an evil disease was to drink heavily, enjoy life's pleasures, and go about singing and having fun."

Still others pursued a middle way, "neither restricting their diet so much as the first group, nor letting themselves go in drinking and other forms of dissipation so much as the second, but doing just enough to satisfy their appetites." A last group believed, as did the characters in his book, that "no medicine was better or more effective against the plague than flight." Even fleeing didn't always work; Boccaccio wrote that "many proponents of each view got sick here, there, and everywhere." And over half of those who became ill died.

Medicine then was still guided by Galen's notion of humors. The sick might be purged or bled; or they might be prescribed medicines to balance their humors, or strengthen their organs, or neutralize toxins. Some of the remedies were foods and herbs, including onions, of course, along with garlic, borage, angelica, and rue. The best-known remedy was theriac, a blend of many—sometimes as many as eighty—herbs, foods, and natural medicinals. Whatever the individual recipe, theriac always contained a fair bit of opium. A plague treatise from 1348 recommended taking "one drachm of fine theriac three times a week, in order to ward off pestilence." The opium would have eased the sufferer's pain, maybe dulled their anxiety, but theriac did not ward off the plague, which continued to rage.

As it had in the Justinian Plague, *Y. pestis* usually attacked the sufferer's lymphatic system. But the Black Death was two pandemics in one. In addition to attacking the lymphatic system, *Y. pestis* could also attack the respiratory system, causing a pneumonia so severe that more than 90 percent of those so infected died in just a few days. Because they had terrible coughing fits, the people who got the pneumonia version spread the virus much farther than those who had buboes, part of the reason that pandemic was so deadly.

SARS-COV-2 IS SIMILARLY prolific. At first, COVID-19 seemed to be strictly a respiratory disease, but since those first few weeks other kinds of symptoms have emerged, including anosmia, heart and blood vessel problems, and the wide cluster of ailments that those with long COVID are reporting. It's as if the virus can locate the host's frailties, attacking where it will do the most damage. But only "as if." Really, the virus is just being a virus, looking for hosts in which it can reproduce, and then copying itself again and again. Our symptoms, our sicknesses, our deaths are collateral damage. I'm not sure if this is a more or less brutal truth than the one people held during the Black Death, believing their god was punishing them with pestilence.

THOUGH IT NEVER fully disappeared, the worst of the Black Death was over by 1353. Reflecting on the plague, which killed both his parents while he was still a teenager, the philosopher Abd al-Rahman ibn Khaldun wrote that it "devastated nations and caused populations to vanish. It swallowed up many of the good things of civilization and wiped them out. It overtook the dynasties at the time of their senility, when they had reached the limit of their duration. It lessened their power. . . . The entire inhabited world changed."

How profoundly the inhabited world changed is difficult to imagine. Estimates suggest Europe lost as much as half its population, and North Africa and the Middle East were nearly as devastated. In all, between seventy-five and two hundred million people likely died due to the plague, at a time when the world's population was only three to four hundred million. Men died more often than women did, poor folks more often than rich. And unlike the Athenian Plague, this one killed children and young people more often than older adults. Urbanites fared worse than rural residents, though the plague also decimated entire villages and towns, killing whole communities in a matter of days or weeks.

Over the next century, Europe's social and economic character changed palpably. Unable to adequately explain to its faithful why the plague happened, the Catholic Church lost some of its power. International trade waned until both supply and demand could rebound. In some regions, tremendous labor shortages enabled workers who remained on the land to demand better pay and conditions. Grain growing was supplanted, in part, by less arduous farming models, like raising sheep and other livestock. Maintaining wealth by charging rents and relying on the labor of tenant farmers became more difficult, so lords of manors gradually parceled out their estates. Peasants had the chance to pay long-term fixed rate leases or even purchase land. By 1500, few traditional manors remained in Europe.

Other peasants moved into the cities, taking up trades. Though they made a living, they often struggled to move beyond the journeyman level, boxed out by families unwilling to share status with the new arrivals. While this arrangement didn't accrue as much benefit to the journeymen as rural peasants were beginning to enjoy, it did require the tradespeople and manufacturers to adopt more market-based practices. The combined effects of the demise of the manors and the increased entrepreneurialism of urban businessmen helped propel the rise of capitalism.

WE'RE ALREADY SEEING some economic effects from the current pandemic. The supply chain continues to stutter, as one item, then another, disappears from store shelves. Tourism has all but disappeared. Will we re-regionalize production to reduce our reliance on global supply chains? Will locales like Venice, places that rely primarily on tourism, need to reorient? And what of the economy writ large? When the immediate danger is finally behind us, will we look at the new world with new eyes?

EARLY IN THE pandemic, my anxious body made so much cortisol I literally shook most days. Even when I wasn't shaking on the outside, my insides felt overrun by scrabbling ants. I actually cut back on coffee for a while. Now, instead of being amped up, I'm exhausted; I feel like I'm sitting on the bottom of a swimming pool, uninterested in surfacing.

I think I may be grieving, though I'm not doing the steps in the "right" order. Even folks like me, who haven't lost a beloved person, have plenty to grieve: We've lost the world we knew. Looking back at how I felt in March and April, I seem to have skipped over denial and jumped straight to anger. I was enraged not by the virus but by the people who stayed steeped in denial, who were living as though the new reality didn't require any changes to their behavior. Now that I'm thinking about grief and grief stages, I realize many folks were likely in grief-denial, not truculence-denial, which makes me regret some of my fury.

Though I didn't recognize it at the time, I think I was hurrying past the unpleasant grief emotions, rushing to acceptance. I poured attention and energy into growing a garden full of food, started learning everything I could about viruses and pandemics, organized the community COVID task force. When public health professionals urged everyone to help "flatten the curve," I leavened in a dose of bargaining, not with God or the virus, but with myself. "They're predicting the curve could be flat by my birthday. Stay home until them. It's no big deal, just a few months," I assured me. But my birthday was last month, the curve isn't flat, and I'm so tired I think I may be depressed, backtracking to yet another grief step I skipped.

I have to force myself to see people, even my closest friends. I tell myself these visits are double, time together now and warm memories to conjure this winter, when it's too cold to visit outside. Laura, one of my best friends, came by today. She brought her whoodle, Betty, fifty pounds of pure enthusiasm. Normally, Betty says hello by joyfully assaulting me, grabbing at my wrists and holding them lightly between unbiting teeth, then trying to lick my arms and feet. But today, Laura leaves her in the car, as we're not sure what animals can carry the virus.

Laura and I don't hug hello. She lifts up a small sack, says she brought her own glass and wine. I get a drink for myself, and we head to the side lawn, to a gentle rise pocked by a faint lattice of hollows, the last traces of the orchard that almost was. Rob and I never put chairs there before, but with the world reduced to house and yard, I moved a pair there the other day. I've been testing out different places to sit, looking for different views. Once Laura and I get settled, my melancholy lifts and I'm glad we're together. The oddness then is how normal I feel, how ordinary our chatter and laughter are. For an hour or so, it is summertime in Maine, the sun so bright we block its glare with cupped hands, the grass alive with pests we don't much mind, the air cloyingly sweet with diesel fumes from lobster boats. For an hour or so, all manner of things are well.

DR. FAUCI SAYS he's optimistic a vaccine will be available in the first quarter of 2021, which would be incredible. Still, that's at least five more *quarantina* away, with three of them during the coldest, darkest part of the year here.

A WEEK AGO, I spotted the first corn tassel, and within days, dozens of shaggy filaments were swaying gently atop the stalks. This is the third year I've tried to grow corn. The first two times, the plants did beautifully until August. Then, the remnants of some hurricane arrived, and the corn plants were battered beyond their ability to bounce back. Their stalks were snapped, and their leaves became glazed with salty water.

Now that we have a greenhouse, I decided to try corn again. Not that I was planning to grow corn in it, as corn has deep roots and does far better when grown in a grid rather than in a single long row. No, my plan was to plant the corn in five-gallon paint buckets and put them *behind* the greenhouse, using it as a buffer to protect them. Which I did, in fact, back on May 2. I filled nine big buckets with a little loam and a lot of compost and put several kernels of a stunningly beautiful cultivar called Wade's Giant Indian Flint Corn in each one. It has ears a foot long and kernels that are deep yellow, cream, purple, lavender, lilac, and rust. Once the kernels were planted, I set the cans in the lee of the building, confident it would protect them from ordinary wind gusts. Whenever a storm was predicted, I planned to move them closer to one another and to the greenhouse for extra protection.

As in other years, the plants got off to a great start. The first kernels germinated on May 8, and they've grown well since.

Once the tassels arrive, it's usually about three weeks until the silks on the cobs begin to dry out and turn brown, a sign the kernels are mature. So, sometime after August 18, I expected the corn would be ready.

Alas, my plan went triply awry. The growing guide I'd followed recommended putting four or five kernels in each can, which turns out to be a bad idea. Corn needs to keep its friends close, but not that close. Plants are less likely to form mature cobs if they feel cramped, meaning I was in for a smaller harvest than I'd hoped. Plus, I'd neglected to check whether Wade's Giant is a good option to plant in a container. Had I looked, I'd have learned the National Gardener's Association believes it is not. So, when Hurricane Isaias arrived on the night of August 3 and upset a third of the cans, the tall, hefty stalks that toppled over not only broke, they broke the other stalks they fell onto. Salt water filled the cans that remained upright. By the time Isaias headed out to sea, the corn was unsalvageable.

Such bouts of agricultural incompetence frustrate me, of course, but they also heighten my awe at the earliest agriculturalists, who figured out how to turn wild plants into reliable staples, improving them in whatever ways they most valued. They did it all without the benefit of internet advice, agronomy, or (often) written language.

THE VERY-GREAT-GRANDMOTHER OF Wade's Giant Indian Flint Corn and all other corn was teosinte, a grass native to Central America that the Mayan people began domesticating sometime between 6,200 and 9,000 years ago. Unlike contemporary corn, teosinte is bushy, with several stalks. Like corn, it has a male tassel at the top of each stalk and female ears tucked against the stalk, partway up. But teosinte ears are small, just two or three inches long, with a dozen or fewer kernels, whereas corn ears can be over a foot long with as many as five hundred kernels. Teosinte kernels have hard fruit walls rather than the delicate, paper-thin, soft fruit walls of sweet corns. Domesticating teosinte involved gradually selecting for all the attributes that people value in corn, including the bigger, sweeter, softer kernels and larger cobs.

In his book *Maize for the Gods*, Michael Blake conjectures the first mutation that hunter-gatherers noticed was that some teosinte cobs didn't shatter when ripe, much like the nonshattering wheat and rye spikelets other hunter-gatherers noticed in the Fertile Crescent region. As was the case for those grasses, teosinte plants with cobs that didn't shatter couldn't self-propagate; they needed an animal to sow their seeds. Hunter-gatherers helped with that task. While doing so, they also extended the variant's range by sharing gifts of seed with trading partners. Over time, teosinte-maize traveled throughout Mexico, into the southwestern part of what is now the United States, east to the Caribbean Islands, and farther south into Central and South America. By the times it was fully corn, plants were present in much of North and South America.

The transformation of teosinte into corn happened in two major waves. Sometime between seven thousand and four thousand years ago, corn became an edible crop, but it didn't become a staple until later. Starting around three thousand years ago, during the second wave of concerted breeding, new varieties emerged as corn coevolved with its new locales and growers selected for greater productivity. Blake calls this process "biosocial entanglement" because people and plants "become trapped in one another's webs of action and response, both behavioral and genetic."

I LOVE THIS notion. While "domestication" implies the domesticator species is in charge, determining how the domesticated species changes, "biosocial entanglement" is more clearly mutual. Being trapped in one another's webs, people and plants influence each other.

I'm definitely trapped in plenty of plants' behavioral webs. I planted daffodils I didn't especially want to keep the deer at bay. I added traps for Japanese beetles to protect the raspberries. I spend untold hours weeding. I give the tomatoes planted in grow bags drinks of milk to make sure they get enough calcium. The garden plants even determined, in the Before Times, when I could take trips. I almost never went away for more than a few days between late March and early October, as I didn't want to leave them untended. They quietly boss me around, letting me know when they want more water or less, when they need more nutrients, when they want to be pruned. The plants want care and attention, and I give them what I can. The flip side, of course, is that I want the plants to thrive so we can eat them.

Such are the tangled webs we weave, the networks of mutual obligation in which we dwell.

FOR MAYANS, CORN remains sacred, thoroughly woven into their biosocial webs. Their creation story, the Popol Vuh, teaches that the deities created humans out of a combination of white and yellow corn. As Mayans and other Mesoamericans traded and migrated, some carried corn south from Mexico to South America, where it became a sacred drink. Fermented, it's chicha, "a drink from and for the gods." Other migrating peoples carried corn north, where it became a staple food crop. Corn became so important to the Puebloan peoples that they, too, regard it as sacred.

THE COLORFUL FLINT corn I tried to grow isn't eaten fresh. With hard kernels and less sugar than sweet corn, flint corn is better suited to making meal and flour. Though originally cultivated in a far different climate, flint corns were an important crop in Maine for centuries, grown first by the Abenaki and later by European settlers. Then, during the 1800s, flint corn was supplanted almost entirely by sweet corn.

For thirty years, a seed-saver and corn keeper named Albie Barden has been working to reintroduce flint corns to Maine. Barden feels a strong connection to the region's Native heritage and sees saving flint corns as a way to begin redressing the harms settlers caused to Indigenous populations. He also hopes doing so will help people establish "a sacred relationship to the land and the plants," one putting us "on a healing path of right livelihood with the Earth." Barden's flint-corn journey began in earnest when he was leading a class on plant medicine and a participant gave him twelve kernels of Abenaki Rose flint corn, a lovely cultivar with a creamy undercoat and deep-pink caps on each kernel. Barden took the gesture to heart. He knew Indigenous herbalists believe that when plants come into your life unexpectedly, they are offering you a chance to learn something you need to know. He planted the kernels, and all twelve germinated. At the end of the first season, he had twenty-three ears of corn. From them, he "started to do a fairly significant giveaway of Abenaki Rose, with the idea that it was kind of a calling to preserve the ancient varieties of flint corn and to make sure they survive." In the years since, Barden has grown and given away enough Abenaki Rose flint corn that it's relatively plentiful now, available from several specialty seed farms and even sold on Etsy.

I THINK OF such seed-saving as a kind of redemption. It can, as Barden hoped, put folks on a healing path with the earth, can remind us of our sacred relationships to other beings. In some ways, it's the obverse of domestication: rather than tweaking the traits of another being to make it more congenial to us, we make ourselves stewards of that being, just as it is. A horticulturalist might point out that seed grown in new circumstances will often produce a plant different from its forebears, and she'd be right. But seed-savers do what they can to maintain at-risk germ lines, to preserve life-forms that would otherwise be lost.

EVERY YEAR, I buy some of my seeds from Seed Saver Exchange, an organization established in the 1970s as a collaborative, grassroots seed bank. The early participants wanted it to be a fail-safe—a store of genetic biodiversity in case something dire happened to the USDA germ banks, which were then so underfunded they struggled to fulfill their mission. The Exchange is now the largest nongovernmental seed bank in the country, home to more than twenty thousand different types of seeds.

While some seeds arrive there with provenance and backstories, many come without documentation—not a stub of a migration story, not a picture, not even a description of the plant. Last winter, the Exchange put out a call for volunteers to expand the entries of some of these undocumented seeds. I offered to grow five kinds of beans. As I had nothing else to go on, I chose an alphabetical run, requested Angie's, Blue Boy, Cambridge, Double Hull, and Echo IV.

The seeds and I got off to a promising start. I was happy to discover they looked a good bit different from each other. Angie's look a lot like Taos beans, varying shades of café au lait. Blue Boy is not blue; it's white and flattish. Cambridge is the most unusual: two-thirds of the beans are white, the other third dark blue—something Gregor Mendel could no doubt explain. Double Hulls are quite shiny, their medium-brown coats streaked with darker brown, while Echo IV looks like a regular turtle bean, blue-black and matte. I planted them the second week of June, and almost all of them germinated. A month later, I spotted the first few vine tendrils twirling away from the leaves. After a few more days, the first furled flowers appeared. But before those flowers had a chance to open, the bold, hungry doe who ignored all the antideer measures of *Operation*

Beautiful Deterrence browsed them, nibbled every single plant down to its lowest leaves.

IN 2008, I discovered an alliance called Renewing America's Food Traditions. It makes food lists for North America; each includes the foods that were historically important to a given region but are now endangered. The list for our region, which encompasses New England and the Maritime Provinces, helped give some shape to my general curiosity about heirloom seeds. While I do grow heirlooms that aren't from this region, I always include plants that are. Over the years, I've grown lots of regional beans: Bumble Bee, King of Early, Lazy Housewife, Maine Yellow Eye, Mayflower, Marfax, True Red Cranberry Pole, and Vermont Cranberry Bush have all had a place in our garden. We've also grown Boothby Blond cucumbers, Early Chantenay carrots, Marrowfat peas, Green Mountain and Katahdin potatoes, and Large Red and Orange Oxheart tomatoes.

EVEN AS I strive to preserve regional plants, I try to hold in mind that plants and people are recent arrivals to this place, that dry land itself is relatively new. Twenty-five thousand years ago, what is now Maine was a mile and a half below the Laurentide Ice Sheet. Around twenty-one thousand years ago, when the earth tilted slightly, the region began to warm. The ice slowly melted, and ocean levels rose; what is now Knox County, where Rob and I live, remained underwater for thousands of years.

In fact, most of Maine wasn't above water until around twelve thousand years ago. About five hundred years later, Paleo-Indians arrived. The environment they encountered included wetland sedges and grasses, some deciduous trees, like birch and alder, and some conifers, including spruce. Wooly mammoths, mastodons, and giant beavers were common. The Paleo-Indians disappeared between ten-thousand and eight thousand years ago, perhaps because the environment was changing again. The boreal forests were migrating north, and many archaeologists surmise the Paleo-Indians did so as well to follow their main prey, caribou.

Newly arrived peoples could take advantage of a widening variety of food sources. They gradually transitioned from being true hunter-gatherers to maintaining seasonal homesites. Like the people in the Fertile Crescent who learned to domesticate and cook grains, those in this region learned to grind and mill cereals into flours. They also hunted land animals, birds, fish, and marine mammals.

Around five thousand years ago, sea levels stabilized at roughly their current levels. Another warming period prompted more plants and animals to migrate northward into the region. Little information is available regarding the people who lived here prior to about 3,700 years ago. They may have been Abenaki; certainly, the Abenaki have been in what is now Maine for at least three thousand years. Though the Abenaki became agriculturalists, they continued to fish and hunt to supplement what they grew.

Over the next fifteen hundred years, populations rose for the Abenaki, Mi'kmaq, Maliseet, Passamaquoddy, and Penobscot—who are collectively known as the Wabanaki Confederacy. By 1600, the Wabanaki Confederacy numbered around forty thousand people.

To FOLKS IN our town who can trace their lineage here back generations, I will always be "from away." To members of the Wabanaki nations, my neighbors are also newcomers. In a place like Maine, where all living beings are recent arrivals and where the earliest inhabitants have long since disappeared due to climate changes, the definition of who or what is native and who or what is not depends on how the dividing lines are drawn.

For plants, the US Department of Agriculture has created sensible-sounding but deeply fraught categories. They define "native plants" as those that were in a specific locale before European settlers arrived. "Non-native" plants were brought to a new habitat by people. And "invasive" plants are non-native and "likely to cause economic or environmental harm or harm to human health."

As HARD AS their staffs try to keep hospitals clean, they are awash in germs, which is why I've been avoiding them since March. The only medical appointment I kept was done via Zoom. But I have to go to the oncologist, to the actual office, because I need an infusion. Rob offered to come, which is even nicer than it sounds, as it's almost two hours each way and he would have to wait elsewhere during the appointment.

After promising Rob I truly don't mind going alone, I drive myself. The world through my windshield seems brighter than normal, like an oversaturated photograph. Five minutes before my appointment, as I sit waiting in the parking lot, a text alerts me to come in. The waiting room has been reorganized, now holds half as many chairs and twice as many hand sanitizer stations. A plexiglass divider separates patients from the receptionist. Although I'm wearing a mask, she gives me a new one to wear there. Just a minute or two later, a nurse calls me in to get my vitals checked and blood work done. Instead of sending me back to the waiting room, as in the past, she escorts me to the exam room, where she gives me a disposable johnny rather than a cloth one. After a brief exam, the doctor walks me to the infusion room. In the past, I'd have sat in its waiting area, but today she leads me to an infusion station right away.

This infusion room is spacious, with sixteen stations. Each includes a gray or blue pleather recliner, a straight chair, a small adjustable table, and an IV pole. Waiting for the medicine to wend its way into me, I pay extra attention to the cleanliness protocols—the signs indicating which chairs have been cleaned and are ready for use, the plastic wrappers enshrouding disposable drinking cups, the nurses changing their gloves between patients, the alcohol-soaked wipes they use to clean every lock and connector on the drip chambers and catheters and IV tubes. The main waiting room and the exam room protocols were different than they had been in the Before Times, but nothing seems different in here.

Being in the infusion room usually makes me kind of depressed. In between visits, I think of myself as someone who *had* cancer. But when I'm here, I can't avoid the reality that I'm a cancer patient, present tense. Today, though, I don't mind the antiseptic room and procedures; "Yes," they assert, "you're still a cancer patient." But they also promise, "While you're here, we'll keep you safe."

BEFORE THE PANDEMIC, we were naive—in both the immunological and the usual sense. An immune system is naive if it hasn't been exposed to a specific antigen. The immune systems of newborn babies are naive to most antigens. Those born by C-section are even more naive, as babies who travel through the birth canal are exposed to lots of bacteria there. The Europeans first exposed to syphilis were naive to its source; similarly, Native Americans exposed by colonists to various germs common in Europe were immunologically naive to them. Naivete explains why the syphilis epidemic in Europe and the smallpox epidemics in the Americas were so devastating.

At the beginning of 2020, everyone in the world was naive to SARS-CoV-2 which, likewise, explains why the virus is spreading so rapidly. Our intellectual naivete might have been helpful at first. In March and April, laypeople mostly thought life would go back to normal in a few weeks, a few months at worst. That ingenuousness probably helped people bear the uncertainty and fear. Many imagined the pandemic was a forced hiatus during which they could learn to bake bread or spend more time with family or binge-watch old TV shows. But whatever benefit it may have conferred at the outset, intellectual naivete is now as dangerous as its immunological counterpart.

MAINE IS IN the midst of its first COVID-19 super-spreader outbreak. People who attended a wedding in Penobscot Country on August 7 have been getting sick. Less than two weeks have passed since then, and more than half the guests have tested positive for COVID-19. Many have gone on to inadvertently infect others. A woman who didn't attend the wedding died after being in contact with a wedding guest who'd contracted the virus. Already, it's led to another outbreak miles away from the wedding site.

Few people in Penobscot County had been diagnosed with COVID-19 before August 7. Maybe that gave the wedding party and the guests a sense of false assurance, let them imagine the virus was confined to cities. Maybe the pleasure of being together, celebrating love, made them feel invincible. Maybe they just didn't want to wear masks. But the rippling repercussions, as the virus creates pockets of illness far from the church, show how dangerous such naivete can be.

WHEN THE REST of the yard and garden are fading into fall, it's time to plant garlic. Often, I buy "seed garlic" at the Common Ground Country Fair, an annual fall fair focused on celebrating organic agriculture and sustainable living. Getting it there ensures that the heads haven't been chemically treated to prevent sprouting, as much of the garlic in grocery stores has been. I start by separating the head into individual cloves, leaving the papery protective skin in place. I try to remember to plant them with the pointy side up, though that's less important, I think, than making sure they're at least three inches deep and far enough apart that they'll have room for their leaves and scapes to stretch out next spring. Then I cover the bed with hay mulch. For the next few weeks, before they become dormant for winter, the cloves will put their energy into creating roots. During the winter, their depth in the soil and the layer of hay will help protect them from wild weather. As soon as the soil softens in spring, they'll awaken and sprout. Their first narrow leaves are among the earliest arrivals in our garden.

IT'S NOT YET time to plant garlic; that'll happen at the beginning of October. Now, it's time to harvest the bulbs I planted last fall. The two kinds we grew this season are German White and Spanish Roja. German White bulbs, though twice as large, contain half as many cloves as the small purply Rojas. I've grown German White a bunch of times, but Spanish Roja is new for me. It reached the US in the late 1800s, arriving in Oregon and quickly gaining popularity throughout the Pacific Northwest. The name suggests it's from Spain, and maybe it is. But also maybe not; its other names are Greek garlic and Greek Blue garlic.

Some years, I've waited too long to harvest the garlic, either because I've been otherwise occupied, or the weather hasn't been right. When that happens, the bulbs can break apart; some get wormy before I get around to harvesting. This year, I was here (of course) and noted when the lowest pair of leaves turned brown on most of the plants; I harvested the garlic the next dry day, which was August 10. After setting aside a few bulbs to use soon and a few to plant for next year, we cure the rest. In the dim passageway between the garage and the house, we have a harvest table, an eight-foot-long hand-me-down I cover with cardboard. We spread out the garlic, trying to keep the stalks and leaves from tangling, then ignore them for a few weeks while they dry.

When the leaves are brown and wizened, the feathery paper surrounding each bulb begins to flake. I gently shake each bulb to dislodge the dirt and stones clinging to its thready roots, then I rub dirt off the bulb itself, taking the outer layer of paper with it. Once a bulb seems presentable, I cut its stalk six to eight inches above the bulb and twist off a few papery layers from the remaining stalk so it is nearly the same hue as the bulb. The German Whites look like ghost pipes or pallid lollipops. Someday, I want to learn to make garlic braids.

The Spanish Roja are less uniform than the German Whites. Most are well-formed bulbs with faintly purple paper skins, but quite a few bulbs also have one or two cloves growing outside of that paper skin. I've never seen garlic with extra cloves like this, so I checked my gardening books and searched the internet to find out whether this is a Spanish Roja trait; only one of the photos I found featured a bulb like mine, with extra bonus cloves.

Not having any luck finding an answer, I looked on a USDA site to get the name of their expert on garlic and other alliums and sent her an email. Six hours later, she replied. She said several types of garlic often produce cloves outside the main bulb wrapper. She'd seen it in Creole, Middle Eastern, and Silver Skin types. But she'd never seen it in Spanish Roja, which is a Rocambole type, or in any other Rocamboles. Armed with this new knowledge, I went back online. Silver Skin, it turns out, looks a lot like Spanish Roja. Perhaps my Roja was a mislabeled Silver Skin? But no, Silver Skins are soft-neck garlics, and the garlic I grew is definitely a hard-neck. Perhaps my Spanish Roja contains a mutation. Perhaps it's some other garlic. I don't know. But I do know it's delicious.

IF ALLIUMS WERE the protective, curative superfoods that Hippocrates and Galen and others believed, I could worry less about getting sick. But as I'm pretty sure they aren't, today's news knocked me further off balance. A twenty-five-year-old man just got reinfected with COVID-19. Actually, he didn't *just* get reinfected. He got sick initially in March and was hospitalized until mid-April. Then he got sick again last month. The scientists who sequenced the RNA confirmed the recent strain was a different version of the virus. The man was fortunate and had no symptoms the second time around, meaning his body mustered an immune response and protected him. But, he can still infect other people.

The virus is getting stealthier. We need a vaccine, stat.

THE HEIRLOOM MELONS are ripening. Pretty much every other day, one is ready. The Charentais are splendid, sweet without being saccharine, juicy but firm. The Petit Gris de Rennes are a close second, and Noir des Carmes a satisfactory third. Compared to the others, poor Melone Retato Degli Ortolani, the Italian heirloom, is an also-ran, its flavor as ho-hum as its name.

SPEAKING OF HO-HUM: Joe Biden is officially the Democratic nominee for president. I don't mean that cruelly; I hope he wins. If Trump is re-elected, I'm terrified the combination of the pandemic, his politicizing of it, and his general incompetence will ruin the United States. That's the kind of thing my brother would rail on me for saying. Obviously, I want to be wrong, but in learning about other pandemics, I see many echoes between their thens and our now. Granted, no two pandemics are exactly alike; in fact, those who study them joke that "if you've seen one pandemic, you've seen . . . one pandemic." But the similarities are hard to discount.

Syphilis revealed and exacerbated xenophobia and religious animosities. The Antonine Plague reordered people's sense of time. The Justinian Plague was likely made worse by a leader whose personal weaknesses made him unsuited to that crisis. That plague, as well as the Black Death and the Spanish flu, spread quickly and widely.

Another trait those pandemics shared was tipping an empire toward its demise. The Plague of Athens coincided with the end of their Golden Age. The Justinian Plague contributed a final blow to the faltering Roman Empire. The Spanish flu came at the end of the British Empire. And in *Rolling Stone* this month, the anthropologist Wade Davis described our national response to COVID-19 as "a turning point" for "the international standing of the United States of America." Instead of being a model to other nations, we are flailing. Is the American Era over? Davis believes so, attributes it to our "national obsession" with individualism, which has led us to forsake "not just community but the very idea of society."

AS I THINK about it more, the truism that "if you've seen one pandemic, you've seen . . . one pandemic" seems wrong both because distinct pandemics have traits in common and because a single pandemic is actually manifold. While it may be just one pandemic epidemiologically (and even that isn't guaranteed), it isn't just one experientially. Where in the world you live, whether your nation's leaders act quickly and take strong measures (or not), whether you have enough living space (or not), whether you're an essential worker (or not), whether everyone in your household is relatively healthy (or not), whether you or someone you know has gotten—or succumbed to—COVID-19 already (or not), whether you are relatively well-off (or not), whether you're part of a social group with poor health-care access (or not), even whether your community generally agrees about masks and other safety measures (or not) all contribute to the pandemic's contours.

One virus is causing this crisis, but our experiences are infinitely diverse.

SEPTEMBER

AUGUST INTO EARLY September is the only time the tamaracks seem modest, blending in with the nearby spruces and firs. True, their needles are more luxurious than those of many other conifers, but even that's harder to see this time of year.

The swamp maple is slowly coming into its own, changing color one branch at a time. Green leaves dominate the lowest levels; above them are boughs full of the reddish, orangish, brownish hues of autumn.

SINCE LAST JUNE, when the school year ended, several dozen people here in town have been meeting more than weekly to figure out how to get the kids back into school safely. They've worked on everything from how to get little ones to keep their masks on, to the best way to manage lunch crowds, to socially distanced bus routes, to waste-water testing, to upgrading the HVAC system. The process has been fraught as people's politics and preferences collide—especially when it comes to masks. But now, with the first day of school less than a week away, parents are mostly talking about how much they don't want their kids to be the ones who bring COVID-19 to school, how much they don't want to be (and I'm quoting here) "the jerk who wrecks school" and forces everyone back to learning remotely.

This gives me hope. Admittedly, I take hope wherever I can find it these days. By stretching and twisting it just so, the obsession with individualism that Wade Davis decried can, apparently, approximate concern for community. Even if the motive for vigilance is to not be the jerk who wrecks school, the result will still be that folks are safer.

THIS IS LITERALLY what townspeople—residents of the same municipality—should do. "Municipality" derives from the Latin *munus*, "service performed for the community, duty, work," and *capere*, "assume, take." In a municipality, citizens take on the duty of making the community work, which is a bit tautological, as "community" also derives from *munus*.

As, I was intrigued to find, do "immune" and "immunity." Like "germ," these two terms lost their original significance in the late 1800s, when their early definitions were supplanted by medical meanings. Before "immune" meant "exempt from disease," it meant "exempt from public duty." Those who were immune didn't have to perform any public duties because they were too young or too old or otherwise unable to do so. The rest, those who weren't immune, looked after the immune and one another. When Henry David Thoreau wrote "the village was literally a *com-munity*, a league for mutual defense," he was stressing the linguistic roots of our sense of social reciprocity.

The adults in my town disagree about plenty, but we're a *com-munity* when it comes to defending children.

YESTERDAY, DR. FAUCI predicted there would be a safe, effective vaccine by the end of the year. His prediction timeline is getting shorter!

When I mentioned the good news to Kate, she explained that even if one is ready then, which would be the fastest that a new vaccine was created, ever, it would only be truly game-changing if it could be widely distributed without special equipment. Otherwise, it'd only work in places near enough to the manufacturing sites that it doesn't spoil in transit. And, assuming a vaccine could be transported without spoiling, it would have to be manufactured at massive scale, which will require new infrastructure. Once it's made, someone will have to figure out how to get it to everyone in the US and in the world. Either the federal government will have to create a distribution system, or each state will have to create its own. Countries that don't produce a vaccine will need to be able to get some from countries that do, which will raise issues of vaccine equity. Those will come atop issues of vaccine hesitancy. And if those aren't addressed, the virus will continue to infect people and to mutate, which could lead to variants the vaccine doesn't protect against.

I love Kate. I'm grateful for Kate—always, but especially of late. Still, I wish she'd let me have a little more time to savor this sliver of good news before being brought back to the exigencies of life in the real world, where the situation is grim. The United States just surpassed six million cases. Nationwide, a thousand people are dying from COVID-19 every day. If all of them were in Saint George, the town would be depopulated in less than three days.

I've been making analogies like this one often of late to keep the illnesses and deaths feeling real, to evade the numbing nature of big numbers. Psychologists quoted in the news lately say feeling numb is normal. The acute stress of last spring has become chronic. Our brains can't stay in emotional overdrive for prolonged periods, so they—we—do a reset, come up with a new baseline for what counts as a normal level of stress. We become desensitized so we can cope, which may be good for blood pressure but is not so good for spirits. The loss of feeling doesn't just apply to anxiety. We stop feeling grief and empathy, stop feeling urgency and caution and uncertainty and all the other emotions humans evolved to increase our odds of staying alive.

To remain mindful of the enormity of the pandemic without becoming overwhelmed or inured is the seemingly impossible equilibrium this moment demands.

WITH FOLKS HOME more than usual this summer and able to give their gardens extra attention, local growers are having great yields. People have donated so many fresh vegetables to the community food pantry that we've had a surfeit the last several weeks. The manager added a free market on Friday mornings so none of it would get wasted. Instead of being exclusively for food pantry clients, the free market is open to everyone in town. One at a time, customers come into a small office-turned-produce-mart at the Community Development Center and take as much as they want. They can leave a donation if they'd like, but they don't have to. All that's asked is that they record how many pounds they take.

The manager told me about a tourist who stopped in last Friday. Apparently, she'd seen the sandwich-board sign in the parking lot announcing the free market, and she was upset. She chastised the manager, told her she ought to charge for the food, as it was all local and mostly organic and could generate income for the food pantry. The woman continued at some length, explaining why a free market was a terrible mistake. When at last she wound down, the manager offered her a squash from a heap of gold-and-green striped delicatas and said, simply, "in Saint George, everyone eats."

WHILE I USUALLY have squash and some other vegetables to bring to the food pantry, I seldom have fruit they can use. By the time the apples arrive in our yard, the pantry is already overrun. But this year, we have a banner plum crop, more than enough to use and share with friends, and still have some left to send to the pantry.

Because plum trees blossom early, while it's still cold out, many cultures regard them as symbols of the ability to endure—even to thrive—amid difficult or challenging conditions. And in tree symbology more generally, they are associated with perseverance, hope, and patience.

Our plum tree has those traits. It lives by the garage, the sole tree of its kind amid a stand of spruces. I long assumed it was wild, as no one would deliberately plant a fruit tree in such an inauspicious location. But while researching plums, I discovered "wild" is a specific sort of plum, one with a matte cherry skin. Our plums are a dusky purply-blue, more like Damsons or Brooks or Frenches. Based only on appearance, my vote is French, as the ones on our tree and those pictured online both have imperfect complexions.

I also learned that plums continue to ripen after being picked, which was great news. In past years, we've been able to eat just a few plums before the rest were nibbled or knocked to the ground by some other critter who shares this space. Since I'm here all the time now, I noticed when the plums started to ripen. Rob and I have been picking the ripest every few days.

While I'm an okay cook, I am not a baker. But the world unexpectedly gave us this windfall, and it seems important to honor such generosity. Looking for recipes that require a lot of plums, I chanced on one for a torte that calls for a dozen, far more than any other recipe I saw. It turned out to be easy to make, even for a nonbaker; we shared it with our bubble friends last night.

WHATEVER SORT MY plum tree is, I have Christopher Columbus to thank for it, albeit at many removes. He brought "stones and seeds of European orchard trees" to the New World during his second voyage, hoping that colonists could grow familiar fruits in those very unfamiliar climes. Likewise, on his return, he brought many New World food plants to Europe. Much as the Spice Routes linked disparate regions of Eurasia, Columbus's trips, along with the many he inspired, created new connections between places that had been geographically and biologically isolated from one another. For good and ill, the Columbian Exchange sutured together worlds that had long been separate, (re)creating a single, global whole.

COLUMBUS DELIBERATELY TRANSPORTED foods back and forth, but he also inadvertently carried disease germs, primarily those endemic to Europe. The medical historian Alfred Crosby called the outbreaks caused in the Americas and Africa by these novel germs "virgin soil epidemics," a designation stressing it was the germ's novelty, and not a weakness on the part of those who succumbed, that made the surges so severe. Like Columbus and his crews, explorers and merchants from Europe who came to North America exposed the Indigenous populations to unfamiliar diseases, including smallpox, chicken pox, influenza, and typhoid. Lacking immunity, Native people often got quite sick, and many died.

Here in Maine, an especially terrible disease outbreak began in 1616 near the mouth of the Saco River. It swept through coastal and near-coastal communities and encampments. In just three years, approximately 75 to 90 percent of the Wabanaki Confederacy, as well as of the Nipmuck, Massachusett, Narraganset, Wampanoag, and Patuxet peoples living in what are now eastern Massachusetts and Rhode Island died.

For decades, epidemiologists offered competing and un-satisfying explanations of how this epidemic happened. The symptoms of the most well-known European diseases only partially matched the symptoms and severity of this outbreak. Then, in 2010, a strong contender for the cause was proposed—leptospirosis, a disease caused by the bacterium *Leptospira*. The bacteria are routinely carried by black rats, which traveled in the ships' holds and could easily have come ashore. Once the bacteria reached land, it could infect rodents native to the re-gion; from there, it could enter the soil and water through the infected rodents' urine.

Native people would have been far more prone than Eu-ropeans to getting seriously sick from *Leptospira*, both because they lacked previous exposure and because their lifestyles made re-exposures likely. The bacterium can enter the body through bare feet. It can be ingested from fresh-water streams and ponds, like those where people bathed, and can be inhaled from moist air, like that in a sweat lodge. In a cruel irony, leptospirosis would have been especially deadly for those practicing healing rituals and performing rites for the dead. In contrast, the shoe-clad European traders, who seldom bathed and did not spend time in sweat lodges, were less apt to become ill.

In the wake of the world's re-suturing, virgin soil epidemics were common, especially in the Americas. Their populations fell by nearly 90 percent, dropping from sixty million to just six million. This almost inconceivable tragedy is remembered as the Great Dying.

IN JANUARY 1836, Charles Darwin wrote in his *Journal* that "wherever the European has trod, death seems to pursue the aboriginal. We may look to the wide extent of the Americas, Polynesia, the Cape of Good Hope, and Australia, and we shall find the same result." And yet, as he added, "what renders this fact remarkable is that there might be no appearance of the disease among the crew of the ship which conveyed this destructive importation." Considering several specific incidents, Darwin concluded, "From these facts it would almost appear as if the effluvium of one set of men shut up for some time together was poisonous when inhaled by others; and possibly more so, if the men be different races."

That the crews were "shut up together" may have mattered, but perhaps not. If all were from the same part of Europe, they'd have been exposed to the same diseases, carried the same immunities. Likewise, while race may have mattered to people's susceptibility, it was not so much race itself, but race as a proxy for a population's geographic remoteness from Europe.

THE COLUMBIAN EXCHANGE linked Europe to the Americas and connected both to Africa. Explorers soon realized the soils and climates in many parts of the Americas were well suited to cultivating some important staples, including tobacco, cotton, and sugar. But those arable regions lacked a sufficient workforce, and trading companies and plantation owners were unwilling to pay laborers fairly. Instead, they relied on enslaved people, mostly stolen from Africa. Slave ships traveled a triangular route from Europe to western Africa to the Americas. They exchanged European goods for African people, who were then sold into slavery in South America, the Caribbean, and North America. During this forced migration, more than twelve million African people were stolen.

In Africa, the loss of millions of people depopulated western regions of the continent. Fewer farmers were available to cultivate the fields, leading to widespread famine—which led, in turn, to violence and political upheaval. Despite the desperate conditions at home and the dire ones awaiting them in the Americas, many African women had the conviction and foresight to braid seeds into their hair and that of their daughters before being taken onto slave ships. They wove maize kernels, black-eyed beans, pigeon peas, okra seeds, sorghum, and millet into their cornrows, ensuring themselves access to their ancestral foods. Against nearly insurmountable odds, they had faith that someday they'd be able to grow and eat their native foods.

ON COLUMBUS'S FIRST return trip to Europe, his ships carried a bacterial stowaway, *Treponema pallidum*, which was common on the warm, humid Caribbean islands where he and his crew had disembarked. For centuries, inhabitants of the islands had suffered from rashes and skin lesions caused by *T. pallidum*. Thanks to this lengthy biosocial entanglement, the islanders had some immunity to the bacteria. It seldom made them very ill.

But just as New World inhabitants lacked immunity to diseases like measles and smallpox and leptospirosis, Europeans lacked immunity to *T. pallidum*. When Columbus and crew returned home, some of the crew became mercenaries and joined an army then being created by King Charles VIII of France. These mercenaries carried *T. pallidum*, but because Europe's climate was less warm and less humid than that in the Caribbean, it couldn't live well on most of the body's surface. Instead, it found a home in people's warm, moist genital areas. So rather than passing from person to person via skin contact, as it had in the Caribbean, it began to be transmitted sexually. And because Europeans completely lacked immunity, the bacteria didn't give them minor skin lesions or rashes. Rather, *T. pallidum* caused the syphilis pandemic.

Unpleasant as syphilis can be now, it was far worse early on. Then, "pustules often covered the body from the head to the knees, caused flesh to fall off people's faces, and led to death within a few months." A writer in 1519 described "boils that stood out like Acorns, from whence issued such filthy stinking Matter, that whosoever came within the Scent, believed himself infected. The Colour of these was of a dark Green and the very Aspect as shocking as the pain itself, which yet was as if the Sick had laid upon a fire." The symptoms were so odious that smallpox, itself awful, was called "small" to designate it as *not* syphilis, which was the "great pox."

Over time, *T. pallidum* mutated. In later centuries, the host's symptoms came on more gradually and were less severe, though that change occurred slowly. More than 150 years after the first syphilis epidemic, a British writer included "rottennesse of the periostia and bones; tumours, and sharp pains about the cheekbones, ringing of the ears, clefts of the hands & feet; and grievous tormenting pains throughout the whole body; which becommeth emaciate . . . [and] stinking, loathsome, slimy sweats" as part of a far longer list of symptoms. The abating severity of the disease, while good for humans, benefits the bacteria even more. Since *T. pallidum* moves from host to host through sexual contact, covering the carrier with stinking boils was a poor survival strategy. Far better to make some carriers seem symptom-free, at least initially.

FROM THE OUTSET, SARS-CoV-2 has been able to hide well. Many infected people don't get any symptoms, part of the reason it spreads so effectively. Even so, SARS-CoV-2 has already begun to mutate. One of the spike proteins is different now than in earlier strains. So far, the new strain is worrisome but not terrifying. It infects upper-airways more and replicates better than the earlier strain; however, it doesn't seem more virulent. Evolutionarily, this makes sense; the mutations that help a virus spread are most likely to persist.

YESTERDAY, THE WORLD surpassed thirty million COVID-19 cases. And today, Ruth Bader Ginsburg died. I'm afraid to let myself think about, much less feel, the fullness of this loss, afraid it will undo me. Instead, I am trying to hold on to Henry David Thoreau's observation, maybe even reassurance, that "not till we have lost the world, do we begin to find ourselves, and realize where we are and the infinite extent of our relations." For today, yet again, we have lost a world.

A DECADE OR so ago, I was a volunteer EMT. When we were called to especially bad accidents, I thought a lot about how force could break not just a victim's body, but her entire world. Accidents rupture the timeline, sever the connection between before and after. After a call, I could go home, wash the dishes from the meal I'd abandoned or put the load I'd left in the washer into the dryer, maybe finish grading the student essay I'd been reading. But for the accident victims, their befores no longer portended their afters.

Not only has the pandemic changed how time flows, stretching some days beyond what we feel we can bear, it has eroded the easy assurance that our yesterdays presage our tomorrows. The pandemic will surely ebb eventually; the coronavirus will probably become endemic. Even so, whatever comes next will be different from what was, and different from what would otherwise have been. And we will be different, too.

AT LONG LAST, after taking forever to start to ripen, the tomatoes are arriving en masse. Unless we get a salt-laden storm or an early freeze, I'll be sun-drying tomatoes, blanching tomatoes, and making sauces every weekend until the end of the month.

Putting up food from the garden is a pleasure that's tinged, for me, with irony. For most of my life, first as a student and then as a professor, my year was shaped by the academic calendar. It began not in January but in September. When I began growing food, I thought doing so would reconnect me to the annual calendar and to seasonality. And it has. But like buying seeds in the middle of winter, putting up food takes me out of obvious synch with the season. Instead of spending beautiful early autumn days outdoors, I'm inside preparing for winter.

Until this week, the only tomatoes ripe enough to eat were Cream Sausages and Sungolds. The Cream Sausages were new to me this year; they're paste tomatoes, but are pointier, smaller, and skinnier than most pastes. Happily, they taste like neither cream nor sausage. Their flavor is pleasant, but not strong enough to warrant sun-drying them for later. Sungolds, on the other hand, are a garden staple for us and one of nature's perfect foods; fresh off the vine, they are small explosions of sweetness and acidity. If I exercise self-control and don't eat them all immediately, I sun-dry some to enjoy during winter.

For making sauces, I grow plum tomatoes, which are denser and less seedy than other sorts. But at peak tomato season, when we're inundated with ripe fruit, the beefsteaks, globes, and oxhearts also go into the pot. This year, the full-size tomatoes are Radiator Charlie's Mortgage Lifter, Mark Twain, Red Brandywine, Mamie Brown's Pink, Yellow Brandywine, Dr. Wyche's Yellow Heirloom, Amish paste, and San Marzano.

My medley includes first-timers and old favorites. Radiator Charlie's have been my absolute favorite for the last four or five years; they are huge, sometimes two pounds each, and a deep, dark red. They are sweet, spicy, just acerbic enough, with a hint of umami. If I could only have one tomato, it'd be Radiator Charlie's. But the Mark Twain and Red Brandywine are nearly as good—also big, also deep red, also delicious. Its name notwithstanding, Mamie Brown's Pink is almost as red and beefy as the others. The Amish and San Marzano are both plum tomatoes; Amish are a bit rounder and plumper than many plum tomatoes, while San Marzano split the difference between Amish and the Cream Sausage in shape. The Yellow Brandywine and Dr. Wyche's Yellow Heirloom are both deep yellow, listing toward orange at their darkest.

THOUGH I KNOW they are all heirlooms, I realize I've forgotten everyone's story except Radiator Charlie's, a tomato given to the Southern Exposure Seed Exchange in 1985 by its creator, a radiator repairman named Marshall C. Byles. He crossbred four kinds of tomatoes, repeating the process for six years until he had a stable version that he loved. Others also loved it. He sold seedlings for a dollar each—which was expensive in the 1940s. Doing so, he managed to pay off his six thousand dollar house mortgage in six years.

Once the pot of tomato sauce I've started comes to a slow boil, I turn it down to simmer and sit at the kitchen island looking up the histories of the other tomatoes in the pot. As I skim, I realize why Radiator Charlie's is the only tale I recall; the others have far less detailed backgrounds. Mamie Brown's Pink was given to Seed Saver Exchange in 1995 by Ms. Brown's granddaughter. Yellow Brandywine's provenance is less clear: According to the catalogue copy of the Victory Seed Company, it was "sent to author and tomato authority Craig LeHoullier in 1991 by Barbara Lund of Ohio. She reported that she had received the variety from Charles Knoy of Indiana. Craig subsequently provided samples to Rob Johnston, owner of Johnny's Select Seeds," though "beyond these mentioned facts, the history becomes clouded."

The story attached to the Mark Twain Slicer is cloudier still, and almost certainly wrong. Even so, it's become the default description, appearing in many catalogs. "Odd that a tomato would be named for the famous writer who professed not to like them," one entry begins, before pointing out that Twain wrote "a 1906 story about an unsuccessful 10-hour wild turkey chase in his youth that left him famished and lost in the woods. He rescued himself by finding a garden full of ripe tomatoes. We don't know the history of this obscure heirloom that might be as old as his story." I don't know its history either, but I do know Twain professed—in print—to liking tomatoes very much, as did the fictional character the catalogs cite. The lad in the story says he ate the tomatoes "ravenously, though I had never liked them before," then immediately adds, "Not more than two or three times since have I tasted anything that was so delicious as those tomatoes." Having accurate catalog copy would be handy, especially for a seed sleuth like me, but I bet Mr. Clemens—a consummate conveyor of tall tales and fish stories—would prefer a juicy confabulation to mere facts any day.

I WISH I could simply get a chuckle out of this Twain lore, could appreciate the aptness of its inaptness. Instead I feel disappointed by the realization that not very long ago, someone (likely a lot of someones) knew exactly why the beautiful slicing tomato was called Mark Twain. Now, that knowledge is gone or well-nigh so, and the catalog sketch obscures this lack, making it even more likely the real story will disappear entirely.

WHILE I DON'T know as much as I'd like about the genesis of many recent cultivars, researchers know a surprising amount about the origin of tomatoes themselves. The ancient forebear of tomatoes, like those of corn and potatoes, grew in the Andes. Scientists believe the wild precursor, *Solanum lycopersicum*, was there eighty thousand years ago. Further north, in what is now Mexico, native people began domesticating a wild tomato around seven thousand years ago, crossing its small, blueberry-sized fruits with slightly larger, cherry-sized tomatoes. As the agriculturalists continued to select for qualities they liked, they cultivated larger, smoother-skinned varieties. Early domesticated tomatoes looked like tomatillos, which the Aztecs called *tomatl*, so they called the new fruits *xitomatl*.

The earliest written references to tomatoes are from Spanish colonizers and their retinues, notably those who accompanied the conquistador Hernán Cortés. He'd been sent to the region to claim it for Spain. In 1518, the year before Cortés's army attacked Tenochtitlan, another European explorer landed on Hispaniola and introduced the virus that causes smallpox. Columbus had landed on Hispaniola twenty-five years earlier, at a time when more than three million Taino lived there. The Taino were the largest Indigenous group in the Caribbean, but the diseases introduced by the Spaniards killed many of them within just a few years. Then, over the following decades, the Taino population was further diminished by starvation because the colonizers demanded that native men work in gold mines rather than planting their own crops, as well as by deadly assaults, when men fought back against the colonizers. When smallpox arrived in 1518, it killed almost all the remaining Taino people. Then the virus made its way east to Puerto Rico and west into Mexico, leaving decimated settlements in its wake.

So in 1519, when Cortés and his army attacked Tenochtitlan, the capital city of the Aztec Empire, they faced relatively little resistance from the empire's military forces because so many of them had been lost to smallpox. By 1521, Emperor Moctezuma II had been killed and the Aztec Empire claimed for Spain.

When Cortés returned to Europe, he brought tomatoes from Tenochtitlan. But he didn't know to bring Halictus bees, that plant's sole pollinators, so the only tomatoes to fare well were those with a mutation enabling them to self-pollinate. An early reference to tomatoes appears in an herbal from 1544 where the Italian naturalist Pietro Andrea Mattioli described them as *mala aurea*, "golden apples," suggesting the fruits were yellow. A decade later, when he updated the herbal, Mattioli noted some *mala aurea* were red. In that entry, he also included their vernacular name, *pomi d'oro*, "apples of gold"—which eventually morphed into *pomodoro*.

By the end of the sixteenth century, tomatoes were cultivated in Spain, Italy, Wales, and England, though few were being eaten. Europeans considered their acidity and strong flavors unappealing, in no small part because people often tried the leaves rather than the fruit. Many feared tomatoes were poisonous, which the leaves are if eaten in large quantities. So, rather than being grown as food, the plants were cultivated only as exotic ornamentals and in hope they could be medicines or aphrodisiacs.

The tomato's culinary acceptance was also impeded by the rediscovery, during the Renaissance, of the ideas of the ancient physician Galen. Whereas Galen had been bullish on onions, he would have been decidedly anti-tomato, as it is both cold and wet, making the fruit a poor choice for rebalancing many an imbalanced humor. Renaissance-era botanists considered tomato plants rank, strange, even horrible. Finally, in the seventeenth century, tomatoes begin to appear raw in salads and cooked in other dishes in Spain. By the end of the eighteenth century, they were eaten throughout Europe.

Unlike corn, which traveled directly from South and Central America to North America, tomatoes took the long way around. They made their way to the United States via Europe, carried by French, British, and Spanish settlers. For decades, they were eaten almost exclusively in the southeast. They didn't reach New England or the interior until the late eighteenth century. The brevity of the tomato season, coupled with a lack of preservation methods, limited their usefulness. By 1830, cooks in the United States had developed methods to pickle them and to make preserves and ketchup. As those items suggest, tomatoes were regarded mostly as condiments.

When *Landreth's rural register and almanac* began publishing in 1847, it included only three varieties of "Tomato, or Love Apple" in its seed catalog. David Landreth, the seedsman responsible for the almanac and accompanying catalog, marketed tomatoes almost exclusively to Franco-Americans because other folks in the US would not yet eat them. But just two decades later, the Civil War transformed the tomato market. During the war, soldiers ate lots of canned goods, including canned tomatoes. And in the wake of the war, as canning became economically viable at industrial scale, canned goods became wildly popular. During the last decades of the 1800s through World War II, most of the tomatoes Americans ate were minimally processed canned varieties, the sort sold today as "whole peeled tomatoes."

Plant breeders focused on meeting the demands of large-scale commercial processors, like Campbell's and Heinz, who wanted tomatoes perfectly suited for canning whole. They wanted fruits of uniform size, with a short ripening window, "the right balance of acid and sugar, a thick skin, a deep shape, a rich color, ripening from the inside out and resistance to disease," and the capacity to be harvested mechanically. Breeders at Rutgers University developed a tomato that fit the bill, one that's still available today. Relatively few Americans grew their own in those years, not necessarily because they loved the canned tomatoes, but because the plants then available were cumbersome to tend. They were often mammoth—up to fifteen feet tall with rambling vines.

In the years following World War II, Americans became more interested in eating fresh, rather than canned, tomatoes. And they wanted them year-round. To sate this desire, breeders created hybrids with fruits that matured at around the same time; that were hardy enough to withstand being warehoused and transported; and that were easy to pick. Choosing for those traits, not for flavor, led to the tomatoes of my childhood: three-packs of small, hard, only-mostly-ripe, bland fruits nestled in a plastic crib and covered in crackly cellophane. Eaters eventually balked. Interest in heirloom tomatoes took off in the 1970s, energized by back-to-the-landers who sought and grew healthy food; by the 1990s, an appreciation of heirloom tomatoes had gone mainstream. Today, they are among the most popular plants in home gardens.

PLANT TRAITS TEND to change slowly unless a breeder steps in and manipulates the process. In contrast, language can change quite rapidly, as the meanings of words or their frequency of use shifts due to new circumstances or needs. Yesterday, an article about language trends during the pandemic was published on the website The Conversation. To my surprise, the only truly new English word the pandemic has spawned so far is COVID-19. Much less surprising is that many formerly uncommon words and phrases, along with some novel blend-words, are now in wide use. I expected "pivot," the word I'm guilty of overusing more than any other, to be on the list. But it isn't—at least, it isn't yet.

Back in January, just eight of the top twenty words of the month were pandemic-related; they were familiar words like "virus," "respiratory," and "flu-like." By February, fourteen of the top twenty words were linked to the pandemic; that list included the new coinage "COVID-19," along with "nCoV" and "self-isolate." By March, all twenty of the top keywords were pandemic-related, and included "PPE," "sanitizer," and "lockdown." April added, among others, "frontline" and "hydroxychloroquine"; May, a month marked by more optimism, included "reopen" and "easing," while June intermixed words related to the death of George Floyd with others connected to the pandemic. That grimmer list was topped by "defund," with "brutality" and "racism" not far behind.

The word "non-essential" made the top twenty in both March and April. While it has apparently ceased to be top of mind for others in the months since, I'm still thinking about "non-essential" and its counterpart, "essential," quite a bit. The pandemic has largely upended who Americans count as essential—and who we don't. Some of those we've long considered essential, like doctors and nurses, have retained that designation. But since March, many folks whose positions are more likely to offer low pay, poor benefits, and limited work autonomy—including migrant agricultural workers, grocery store clerks, meatpacking plant workers, hardware store employees, trash collectors, and child care workers—have been touted as essential. Athletes, actors, comedians, and musicians, among others with esteemed jobs, have suddenly become less so.

If I could believe this inversion would stick, that when essential no longer means "you have to risk your life for those who don't," we will still revere grocery store clerks as much as we do professional athletes, I might welcome this linguistic shift. But already, the nightly rounds of applause and songs for essential workers are waning.

IN THE BEFORE Times, "essential" only sometimes modified "worker." More often, it meant "intrinsic to one's being," that without which something isn't itself—a definition gradually broadened to mean "absolutely necessary" more generally. Now, in chronic risk-assessment mode, we ask ourselves daily whether something is important enough to risk sickness to have or to do. Is it absolutely necessary or can I live without it? How much can we pare away and still feel like ourselves? Still be ourselves?

TODAY, SEPTEMBER 28, the one millionth person died from COVID-19. In a *New York Times* article marking it, the author noted that preventing further catastrophe depends on "wide-scale testing, contact tracing, quarantining, social distancing, mask wearing, providing protective gear, developing a clear and consistent strategy, and being willing to shut things down in a hurry when trouble arises." Doing some but not all these things won't work, he says, quoting a scientist from the National Institutes of Health who explained that "it's all an ecosystem. It all works together."

It's *all* "all an ecosystem."

OCTOBER

TODAY, OCTOBER 2, President Trump tested positive for COVID-19, as did the First Lady. On the one hand, of course he did; he's flaunted his refusal to take any safety precautions since the beginning of the pandemic. On the other hand, I thought surely someone must have the secret job of keeping him away from the riskiest of high-risk situations. Apparently not. The Trumps weren't the only ones connected to the White House to test positive. Quite a few other folks who attended a Rose Garden reception for Amy Coney Barrett, the nominee to replace Ruth Bader Ginsberg on the Supreme Court, also fell ill.

THE TWO ANTIQUE rosebushes a friend gave us when we moved here are lovely, but they're fussy plants, and I don't give them as much care as they need to thrive. They do flower every year, but not prolifically. So I was shocked when a second round of roses bloomed this week; they've never bloomed in the fall before.

Seeing their pink petals makes me feel even guiltier about how sick I am of being stuck at home. I'm beyond lucky to have a yard where food and flowers grow. Lucky I can work from home. Lucky to have a partner who does the risky errands. But as the foliage fades and the edges of my world come back into clear focus, I can't help thinking even a luck-gilded, rose-bedecked cage is, in the end, still a cage.

PRESIDENT TRUMP SPENT several days in the hospital, where he received a variety of experimental treatments, including one that was approved less than a week ago. By October 8, thirty-four people who'd attended the Rose Garden event tested positive for COVID-19.

WE'VE STOPPED QUARANTINING our mail and washing our groceries. Occasionally, I go to the post office now, though Rob still does all the food shopping, well, all except for the apple shopping. This year, we joined an heirloom apple CSA. After Rob confirmed how safe the pickup site is, I took over getting our apples. Every other Tuesday, I drive to the Unitarian Church in Rockland, where I pick up a paper bag with my name on it that's sitting on the grass just beyond the parking lot, one of a dozen or so bags beneath a generously canopied tree. Even with this self-serve model, everyone is required to wear a mask. Listening to NPR on the car radio during the hour the trip takes feels so nostalgically normal, so like errand-running of old, that I relish the drive almost as much as the fruit.

Each share includes half a dozen or so different apple types. In September, they were a mix of crab apples and early ripening apple cultivars. But this week, our haul is all full-sized fruits, a King of Tompkins County, a Twenty Ounce, and a few each of Melrose, Opalescent, Prima, Smokehouse, and Spartans. I don't love them all, but most are good. A few have been great, including Smokehouse and one from two weeks ago called Wealthy. My friend Laura also loves apples, so we share them and compare notes on flavor.

The only ripe apples in our yard are the crab apples; sadly, they're tiny, tart, and terrible.

ALMOST SINCE THE outset, conspiracy theorists and a few serious speculators have insisted SARS-CoV-2 originated at the Wuhan Institute of Virology. Most who believe that blame its emergence on a lab accident, though a minority suggest it was released deliberately. They say if SARS-CoV-2 didn't come from that lab, where similar viruses are studied, then finding it first in Wuhan is just too much of a coincidence. I agree it probably isn't a coincidence that the virus emerged where it did, but I don't assume it came from the lab.

In 2012, the science writer David Quammen predicted a pandemic would happen soon, that it would probably be caused by a coronavirus, that the virus would probably come from a bat, and that the initial outbreak would probably occur near a wet market in China—like the one in Wuhan where

SARS-CoV-2 was first found. Quammen isn't a psychic; he was steeped in research he'd done for his book *Spillover: Animal Infections and the Next Human Pandemic.* Like the scientists he shadowed, Quammen believes the new coronavirus originated in a horseshoe bat. While living in the bat, it would have been in the company of many other viruses, including the one that causes SARS.

Since the SARS outbreak in the early 2000s, researchers who focus on links between human health and wildlife health have worried another bat-borne virus would jump to humans. These infected bats aren't traveling to towns and cities on their own; rather, people are going to wild places where the bats live. Quammen points out that "wild landscapes harbor so many species of animals and plants. And within those creatures, so many viruses. We cut the trees, we kill the animals or cage them and send them to markets. We disrupt ecosystems and we shake viruses loose from their natural hosts. When that happens, they need a new host. Often, we are it." And, as we've seen for millennia, once a virus enters a human host, it goes wherever the host does. What once traveled only at the speed of feet or hooves or sail-powered ships can now move as fast as a plane, can cross the globe in less than a day.

Quammen says the best way to reduce the risk of viruses jumping from some other species to humans is to stop impinging on wild ecosystems. He urges folks not to visit such places and to avoid products that use materials found in wild locales. The only wild places I've been are the Galapagos Islands, which Rob and I visited in 2014. Officials there take great care to protect the distinct ecosystems. Before we were allowed to deplane on arrival, the cabin was misted with fumigant. As we walked from the plane to the small terminal, our shoes squelched on a carpeted pathway suffused with sanitizer. Our luggage was misted with more fumigant when it reached the baggage claim area. We traveled between islands on a small boat; before and after each visit to a new place, our shoes were disinfected.

Since the Galapagos Islands generate mostly photographs, not rare gems or minerals or such, I felt relieved and, I admit, a little virtuous knowing I wasn't contributing to habitat destruction or accidentally inviting novel viruses into the wider world. Then, I came to the paragraph where Quammen pointed out that everyone who uses a cell phone is implicated. Cell phone capacitors contain coltan, which is mostly mined in wild, unique ecosystems. The mines damage those ecosystems and the miners encounter—and often eat—the local fauna, including monkeys and bats.

THE DIFFERENCE BETWEEN September and October in a Maine garden is immense. September is a time not just for tomatoes, but for the last great burst of productivity for many of the plants. Now, almost everything is finished for the year. Among the herbs, the sage remains gorgeous and harvestable, and the marjoram and oregano and thyme, despite having gone to flower, are still piquant enough to pick and dry. In our vegetable beds, only jalapeño peppers, carrots, drying beans, and storage potatoes remain. Every day or two, I bring in the jalapeños that have reddened. I'll harvest the storage potatoes this week, and the beans if it's dry enough. The carrots, on the other hand, will remain in the ground as long as possible. Unless we get a hard frost, I won't pull them until early December.

UNLIKE OUR CAREFUL grabbling for early red potatoes, harvesting the storage potatoes is brutish. Rob spades as deeply as he can, lifting and flipping shovelfuls of soil, hoping not to slice through potatoes in the process. I follow in his wake, on hands and knees, reaching for bits of tan in the dark soil or plunging my bare hands into the loosened dirt in search of hidden tubers. Sometimes, a potato collapses in my hand, oozing rottenness faster than I can fling it away. Far more often, I nab a whole, hale potato, carefully toss it onto the adjacent bed.

When we finish, we gather the keepers and bring them into the pass-through. There, we lie them in a single layer atop a piece of cardboard on the harvest table, where the garlic was a month ago. Then, we put another piece of cardboard on top to ensure that air can reach the tubers, but sunlight can't. Too much light turns potatoes green, a sign that they've produced solanine, one of the toxins the ancient Andeans ate clay to counteract. As potatoes were domesticated, growers must have selected against those with a lot of solanine, as they only produce it now if they're stored somewhere with too much light.

ON OCTOBER 14, we got four inches of rain! More than in August and September combined. It felt marvelous, at first, seeing and smelling the drenching rain, but even parched ground can't absorb that much at once. It's puddling in places, sogging the pots of herbs and edible flowers. I'm glad we have so few vegetable plants left in the garden, extremely glad we pulled all the potatoes the other day. The remaining bean plants are bedraggled; even the peppermint, which I think of as nearly indestructible, was bowed by the rain.

So far, the biggest effect of climate disruption in our corner of Maine seems to be changing weather patterns. Winters are less snowy; summers are less predictable. The normal of before, with mostly dry Mays followed by cool, damp Junes, then Julys and Augusts with idyllic days in the high 70s or low 80s, has given way to more erratic conditions. During August and September, we used to get enough rain that I only needed to water the greediest plants. This year, I needed to water everything every day. We have a deep well and a rainwater catchment system, but as the drought wore on, I worried we'd run out of water, and so gave the plants the bare minimums they needed.

LAST YEAR, MAINE officially began marking Indigenous Peoples Day, rather than Columbus Day, on the second Monday in October. I'm glad we're no longer honoring Columbus with a holiday. He didn't "discover" America, and certainly didn't discover what is now the United States. Plus, he treated the Indigenous peoples he did encounter despicably. Even so, I'm uncomfortably reluctant to completely cancel him. To be clear, I'm horrified by the atrocities Columbus and his crew committed. And I grieve the losses of lives, of languages, of cultures, that colonialism has caused in North America and around the world.

But I know, too, that the majority of those who died in the wake of the Columbian Exchange were felled not by deliberate actions by Columbus, but by exposure to novel, disease-causing germs people of that era didn't understand.

The propensity for movement that prompted early *Homo sapiens* to spread across six continents also propelled the era of exploration that was made possible by sailing ships and improved maps. Had it not been Columbus, it would have been Vasco da Gama or Ferdinand Magellan or some other navigator whom we remember for resuturing the continents into a global whole. And any one of them, like Columbus and like the traders who came to the Americas in his wake, would have introduced European diseases.

LESS THAN A century after Columbus's explorations, the human population began a hundred-year-long stretch of rapid growth. This increase was so pronounced it has only two precedents: when our ancestors developed tools and when they became agriculturalists. Changes of such magnitude have many causes, but chief among them in this instance was a broader access to enough food. Columbus introduced horses and Old World livestock to the Americas and many New World plants to Europe and Africa. The horses, which expanded hunting ranges, and the livestock enabled people to consume more protein. And several of the plants introduced into Europe and Africa, notably potatoes, sweet potatoes, beans, corn, and manioc, became staples that gave poor people on those continents better chances for survival.

IN 1539, A friar who accompanied Pizarro's party in Peru described potatoes as "something like Spanish truffles, aside from being a bit bigger and not as tasty"—the first written account of "papas," as the Incas called them. Despite that lackluster assessment, Spaniards introduced potatoes to Europe, Costa Rica, Guatemala, and Mexico over the next several decades. Europeans were skeptical, as they had been about tomatoes. Herbalists in the sixteenth and seventeenth centuries warned that potatoes could exacerbate damp humors, so recommended they should be complemented by hot or drying ingredients. Even in Ireland, a nation whose fate is tied to this tuber, the potato was reputedly just a curiosity at first.

But, as Henry Hobhouse explains in *Seeds of Change: Six Plants that Transformed Mankind*, conditions unique to Ireland primed its residents to embrace the new food: "If the Irish had united in a hegemonous country, if there had been a feudal system founded on land, instead of tribalism based on personal loyalty, if sheep and cattle had not been favored over grain, if the Irish church had not been so disorganized," then Ireland's history would have unfolded differently, because "the right conditions for the adoption of the potato would not have existed." Of course, the history of Ireland *was* as it was, and conditions *were* right for the Irish to adopt the potato.

In the wake of a Catholic-led rebellion in Ireland, Oliver Cromwell led an invasion in 1649 to re-take the territory for England. Under his leadership, land owned by Catholics was taken from them, and they were forced out of towns. The only land available to them was marginal, rocky, boggy, or otherwise poorly suited to growing food. Many—some estimates are as many as half—died.

One food plant that could grow in the poor soil to which the Irish had access was the potato. Potatoes are a virtuous crop. They require less water than do cereal crops like wheat. They're also efficient; a field planted in potatoes can provide more than twice as much protein and three times as many calories as would the same field planted in wheat. And once the foliage dies back, a field full of potatoes looks like a field full of nothing—making it harder for enemies to destroy the crop, or for landlords to demand a share, or for churches to insist on a tithe.

No wonder the potato became a staple. In the late 1600s, 40 percent of the Irish ate no solid food except potatoes. Though monotonous, a diet of potatoes and a bit of milk can provide all the proteins humans need. By 1740, the ordinary Irish diet had expanded, but not by much: most people ate potatoes, milk—and grains. That year, inclement weather destroyed the potatoes that had been overwintering in the ground and ruined the grain season. Famine killed somewhere between 13 and 20 percent of the population during what is known as "the year of the slaughter." Then, thanks largely to the continued reliance on potatoes, Ireland's population ballooned for the only time in its written history. After five centuries of extremely slow growth, the number of Irish tripled in a single century.

Potatoes were similarly critical to feeding people in Europe, and by the end of the eighteenth century, the population on the continent also rose. The crop historian Jonathan Sauer wrote that "the potato temporarily gave continental Europe a vastly increased supply of cheap food, reducing chronic starvation and allowing the population explosion associated with the Industrial Revolution." Hindsight may prompt us to consider the population explosion a mixed blessing, but for those who didn't starve to death, I imagine it was far more a blessing than otherwise. Millions of people were born, lived to adulthood, and had children who would not have done so if Columbus— or someone like him—had not introduced foods poor people could afford.

Were it not for those potatoes, then on the western edge of Ireland, in County Mayo, in the tiny town of Louisburgh, it's quite likely either Thomas Grealis (who was born in 1794) or Rose McGrath (who was born in 1806) would not have been born, much less lived to adulthood. If one or the other didn't get born or didn't grow up, they obviously wouldn't have been able to marry. In that case, James Grealis would not have been born, could not have married Maria A. O'Malley. An unborn James would not have migrated to the United States, could not have had a daughter named Minnie. An unborn Minnie Grealis could not marry Charles O'Toole, would not have had a daughter, Catherine. The unborn Catherine O'Toole, in turn, would not marry Patrick Morrison or become mother to Patricia. And had there not been a Patricia Morrison to marry a Leonard Kelley, there'd be no me.

WHEN THE CONQUISTADORS first brought the potato to Europe, they managed to leave behind its pathogens. But those germs eventually made their way across the sea, and the new cultivars were as susceptible to them as their South American precursors had been.

Fusarium caeruleum, a fungus that causes dry rot, arrived in the 1750s. Harvested potatoes shriveled up in a matter of weeks or months, leaving root cellars empty months before the spring crops were ready. Aphids carrying leaf curl arrived in the 1770s. A mold, *Botrytis cinerea*, was first reported in 1795. Blackleg, an especially pernicious disease caused by a bacillus, destroyed crops and the soil where they'd been grown, beginning in 1833. Then, in 1845, *Phytophthora infestans*, the source of late blight, reached Europe.

P. infestans is the same water mold that killed so many tomatoes up and down the Eastern Seaboard of the US in 2009. It fares best in cool, damp conditions, and as it moved through Europe in 1845, it did more damage in the north than the south. The initial late blight outbreak began in West Flanders, soon reached Paris, and arrived in Ireland in September. While serious, those outbreaks didn't ruin entire harvests. The following year, in contrast, late blight destroyed all the potatoes growing in Ireland. Amid a mass starvation that lasted from 1846 to 1852, Ireland's population fell by a quarter. A million people died due to hunger, another million emigrated. Nearly two centuries later, Ireland's population still has not returned to its prefamine height.

MAINE MADE IT through the summer and into the fall without a huge number of COVID-19 cases, this good fortune a product, in part, of geography. We have few dense cities and lots of rural communities where people are widely scattered. And while it isn't emotionally easy to stay far away from others, it's physically manageable. I walk to the lighthouse more often now that the summer tourist season is over and I can keep at least six feet from any people I see without difficulty.

But the number of cases and deaths is trending upward nationally, with seventy thousand cases reported the day before yesterday. People on our task force are worrying aloud, wondering whether our good-health luck can hold. And whether case numbers rise here soon or not, can we convince folks to keep being cautious during the long, dark months ahead?

As bad as isolating was in March and April, we had the advantages of timing and ignorance. Lots of folks filled what they thought would be a few housebound weeks with cheerful diversions—baking bread, growing scallions on their windowsills, playing Fortnite or Halo or Animal Crossing. But the allure of those activities, like the appeal of jigsaw puzzles, Zoom cocktails, and Marie Kondo-ing closets, has long since waned. Plus, a summer of normal-adjacent life lulled plenty of people into believing the pandemic was abating.

We know more and have better resources than we did seven months ago. We know social distancing and masks help. We know we don't need to bleach groceries or quarantine mail. We know that not one, but several promising vaccine trials are happening. Yesterday, both AstraZeneca and Johnson & Johnson restarted their trials; an effective vaccine might be scant months away. But we also know the compounding loneliness of days spent inside, especially when they come after other such days and other such days and other such days.

SINCE I'M HOME nearly all the time, I manage to pick a quart of perfectly ripe arctic kiwis before the birds eat them. About the size of a grape, the fruits have a smooth, edible skin and a sweet punch of fructose flavor much like that of regular kiwis, but more intense. Despite their deliciousness, I've never seen them in a store or even at a farmers market. I suspect two traits make them a bad choice for grocery stores. They need to be hand-harvested, which is expensive. And they're an all-or-nothing fruit. Their flavor at peak ripeness is incredible. But when they aren't precisely ripe—if they're not yet ready or just past—they're bland and firm or squishy and gross.

Though arctic kiwis' other name is "hardy kiwi," they aren't. They are fragile, wouldn't travel well. Thinking about them got me wondering about other produce that isn't practical to get to market. For centuries, lettuces were only sold locally, as they were too delicate to be shipped. Even after trains became a common means of transporting food, lettuces weren't shipped far. When I was growing up, we ate only iceberg lettuce; it was the hardiest variety, with a chilled shelf life of three weeks, so it could be shipped in refrigerator railcars from California and remain fresh for several more days or a week once it reached New England. In the past several decades, other technological advances have made more delicate lettuces easy to ship, and they are now common in grocery stores. Even extremely fragile foods, like raspberries, can now be found year-round in grocery stores. They've been bred for greater durability and packaged for maximum transportability. Maybe the only foods that don't go to market are those that have never been popular enough for plant breeders to tweak their traits.

I GROW A few jalapeño pepper plants each year, but we rarely eat the peppers fresh. What I'm really doing is helping Rob make chipotles. When enough peppers are red, Rob smokes them outside in a wood-fired oven. This year, the plants fared especially well; we have so many peppers he's smoking them in batches and will have plenty to give away. For the first batch, Rob used the last of the applewood our friend Tommy gave us not long before he died. Once the fire was established, Rob moved all the wood to the edges so the logs would slowly smolder.

Smoking is among the oldest food preservation methods. The heat reduces the amount of water in the food being smoked, which increases its longevity. And the smoke permeates it, conferring the antimicrobial and antifungal chemicals found in wood smoke to the food. In the case of jalapeños, smoking also causes their name to change: they become chipotle, a word derived from the Aztec *chīlpoctli*, "smoked chili."

In what is now Mexico, archaeologists have found remains of peppers in the jalapeño family, *Capsicum annuum*, dating back more than seven thousand years. That family includes not only jalapeños, but many of the most widely known peppers, including cayenne, serrano, Aleppo, poblano, shishito, sweet bells, banana peppers, and Hatch and New Mexican chilis. Chilis added vitamin C and a kick of flavor to ancient diets in this region; most of its other staple foods, like manioc, sweet potatoes, and maize, have simple flavors.

After the fall of the Aztec Empire, conquistadors returning to Europe were almost certainly responsible for introducing *C. annuum* to that continent, though some accounts specifically credit Christopher Columbus with bringing jalapeños there. Unlike several of the other New World foods, peppers were an instant hit, quickly disseminated not only across Europe but also into Asia and Africa. Peppers reached the American Southwest when the Spanish arrived in the 1500s. In areas where there was a strong colonial Spanish presence, soldiers and missionaries imposed peppers and chilis on the native people. Even now, diets in those regions reflect that push; they include more peppers and chilis than do the cuisines in areas where the Spanish presence was less formidable.

Despite being forcibly introduced, *C. annuum* have become embedded in the cultural identities of many in the Southwest. Over the last four hundred-plus years of biosocial entanglement, Chile Nativo have coevolved with the people and environment in the Southwest. They have adapted to the state's many soil types, are able to withstand drought cycles, are resistant to diseases and pests, and are able to grow without fertilizers. They have become discrete, unique cultivars. While all have thin flesh, the various cultivars have distinct flavor, heat, and physical profiles. Some are grown by just a single family.

Successive generations reclaimed the Chile Nativo, made it an important component of their diet. New Mexican activist and farmer Isaura Andaluz emphasized the interconnection between Chile Nativo, the Southwest, and its people: Chile "seeds tether us to the land . . . Passed down for centuries among the Native American and Hispanic people, the seeds are carefully returned to the soil, accompanied with a quiet blessing." While the chile's DNA stayed the same, Native and Hispanic peoples remade it, transformed a mundane food into something sacred.

LIKE CHILES, WILD beans were domesticated by Indigenous peoples in what are now South and Central America. Those legumes had much in common with the lentils and grains other early agriculturalists tamed. The beans themselves were small. They didn't germinate consistently. And when the beans did ripen, their pods shattered and the beans scattered. However, by 5000 BCE, four types of wild beans—tepary, scarlet runner, common, and lima—had been domesticated independently in Mexico and the Andes. Of those, I grow only common beans, *Phaseolus vulgaris*. Tepary beans don't do well in our climate, are far better suited for hot, dry places. Scarlet runner beans and lima beans can grow in Maine, but I much prefer *P. vulgaris*. This year, we have Calima and Crockett filet beans, along with Bumble Bee, Marfax, Dark Red Kidney, Tarbais, and Black Coco drying beans (we also had the A through E beans I was growing out for Seed Saver Exchange before the deer destroyed them).

Despite their portability, the *P. vulgaris* of Central America did not migrate north quickly. They reached the southwestern US in 300 BCE and the eastern US around 1000 CE. Archaeologists attribute their slow uptake to a lack of necessity. North American native peoples could get by without beans because they had access to other protein sources, including fish and fowl. But as their populations grew, so did their need for more proteins. They began cultivating beans. Planting the beans with the corn and squash they already grew, farmers were able to grow a nutritionally complete, meatless diet. Those "three sisters" solved the food shortage for a burgeoning population.

FACTS LIKE THAT knock me out, leave me wondering, "How did they know to do that?" The knowledge that beans were delicious and hearty would no doubt have been carried north by the people bringing the beans, people moving north or conducting trade along the well-established routes. But they were unaware of contemporary tenets of nutrition. How did they know beans met the same bodily needs as did fish and fowl? I can't be sure, but I bet they figured it out by taste.

Taste and smell are ancient senses, were helping other creatures to survive long before hominids came on the scene. The ability to recognize sourness is thought to be the oldest, having developed at least five hundred million years ago in vertebrate fish. They relied on it not to sense the flavors of food, but to sense whether the waters in which they were swimming were sour—a sign of dangerous acidity levels. Gradually, the ability to sense the sourness of the environment evolved into the ability to sense the sourness of something ingested.

For many ancient creatures and some contemporary ones, being cold-blooded enabled individuals to slow their metabolisms when doing so was desirable. If food was in short supply, they could literally chill out, reducing their need for more energy as they waited for food to become available. But warm-blooded creatures—humans among them—need to eat frequently. So as mammals evolved, their organs for smell and taste and the brain regions for processing information from those receptors became more finely tuned so that they could more readily identify what was safe to eat.

Early hominids had the same taste receptors as do modern humans; their taste buds recognized sour, sweet, salty, savory/ umami, and bitter. Sweet and salty items provide essential sugars and salts; those found in nature are often safe to eat. A savory flavor usually indicates the presence of protein. Sourness indicates the presence of acid, which was initially a source of danger. But then, around sixty million years ago, our ancestors lost the ability to derive their own vitamin C. They needed alternative sources, which required finding acids they could consume safely. Creatures who could distinguish, either by smell or by a tiny taste, whether plants had safe or toxic acid levels outcompeted those who couldn't. Likewise, those who could distinguish between small and large quantities of bitterness in plants fared better than those couldn't. Our senses, while not nearly as good as those of many other creatures, are as good as they are because hominids whose senses were less good died young. While being able to sense all those flavors matters, humans have more sensors for sweet and savory than for the other three, a strong hint that they're more important. It makes sense: sweetness is a sign something contains sugar, which is essential for producing energy, and savoriness indicates the presence of the amino acids we need to build proteins.

Early hominids ate a raw-food diet of mostly plant material. Getting enough calories required eating for eight to ten hours a day, chewing or grinding foods to make them soft enough to digest. As hominids diverged from other primates, their brains got bigger. They needed even more calories to keep them humming. Curiously, at the same time their brains began increasing in size, their jaws and guts were decreasing in size. That mismatch no doubt made getting enough food extremely difficult—until they learned to eat cooked meat.

Anthropologists emphasize how important cooking, in general, was to our becoming human. It cut down the time required to find, prepare, and eat enough food and made the nutrients in foods more bio-available. Those proto-humans no longer had to graze all day. And it turns out that primates were predisposed to find cooked foods, especially meats, appealing. The savory taste receptors in primates are especially sensitive to glutamate, which is relatively plentiful in raw leaves, once a primary food source. However, glutamate is far—far, far, far—more plentiful in certain other foods, most notably in cooked meat. In *Tasty: The Art and Science of What We Eat,* John Mc-Quaid explains that at "around 300 degrees Fahrenheit, the tightly coiled proteins in the muscle fibers of meats begin to break up and unwind . . . Then amino acids combine with sugars, the start of a chain reaction that spins out thousands of distinct, flavorful chemicals in trace amounts"—and a whole lot of glutamate. When other foods containing similar amino acids and sugars are cooked, those chemical changes also occur. As they do in beans.

WHEN I TRY to imagine how hominids would have reacted when they first ate cooked meat, I think of the first time I saw one of my nieces eat chocolate ice cream. She was a few months shy of her third birthday. As she spooned each sweet mound into her mouth, her body literally quivered. After several minutes focused only on the bowl before her, she looked up. Her face and arms were smeared with ice cream, her eyes glassy with bliss. In a voice as throaty as I've ever heard in a toddler, she said, simply, "Good."

The ice cream excited her taste sensors for sweetness—a lot of them, all at once. They sent messages to her brain assuring it that a more than ample supply of sugar was on the way, which triggered a burst of serotonin. That huge hit of sugar was way more than an early hominid would ever have had such easy access to, way more than her body needed all at once. No wonder she was brimming over with pleasure.

Similarly, our ancestors' umami receptors were tuned to sense glutamate at the levels found in leaves, the amount they needed to survive. They encountered higher levels when they ate fermented fruits, but even those paled in comparison to the levels in charred meat. When hominids first scavenged fire-downed prey, I imagine they, too, quivered with pleasure, overwhelmed by the unexpected surfeit of a flavor their bodies knew to seek.

DURING THE COLUMBIAN Exchange, explorers took New World beans to Africa and Europe. The filet beans Rob is fond of are often sold as "haricot vert" to emphasize their French origins, but they arrived in France in the 1500s after several millennia of cultivation in Mexico. Similarly, some white drying beans tout their great European provenances: In 1528, Pierio Valeriano of Florence began growing some newly arrived *P. vulgaris*. The duke of Florence, Alessandro de' Medici, liked them quite a bit and helped popularize the version we know as cannellini beans. They were so highly prized that when de' Medici's sister, Catherine, married Henry II of France in 1533, her brother gave them a bag of the beans as a wedding gift. In the 1700s, the Bishop of Tarbes began growing a similar-looking white bean that he'd discovered in Spain. He urged local farmers to grow it as well, and that bean, now known as Tarbais, is the go-to bean for cassoulet. But like haricot vert, the beans that became cannellini and Tarbais were cultivated in Mexico—without fanfare—long before they became popular in Europe.

DRYING BEANS ARE the alpha and omega of the plant's life cycle. If enough of mine survive the ravages of deer and weasels and other critters, I save some to plant in subsequent years. The process is nearly identical to that for saving them to eat.

Once the plants are mostly withered and beige, I wait for a dry spell and then gather the pods. If they're damp when picked, they're more likely to mold. Since both pods and plants are tannish-brown, I pull the whole plant and turn it upside down; dangling like earrings, the marcescent pods are easier to spot. Unless I have an incredibly productive crop (which I didn't this year), I put all the bean pods in the same trug, then leave it in the pass-through for a day or two to give the earwigs and pill bugs and other pests a chance to leave. When they are likely gone, I cover the counter with newsprint and begin shucking.

While the five kinds of bean plants look incredibly similar, the beans themselves do not.

Marfax are plump and golden brown, with a tiny dark ring around the hilum, the spot where they were tethered to the pod. Tarbais are pale ivory and flat, as if each bean had been gently squashed. Bumble Bees are comparatively huge, nearly twice as big as Marfax and Tarbais. Their main hue is a bit darker than that of Tarbais, but where Marfax have a pencil thin line around the hilum, Bumble Bees have a maroon-brown splotch. Black Cocos are roughly the same size as Marfax and black everywhere except the hilum, which is whitish. And the red kidney beans we grow are large and elongated, like puffy commas, and range in color from light brown to brick red. Like the amazing array of potatoes in an Andean field, all these beans can be traced back to wild ancestors in Peru and Mexico.

I store most of the beans in jars in the kitchen cupboard; we'll eat them during the winter. But I put the best twenty of each type into paper bags, then into glass jars, then into the freezer, where they'll stay until next spring. They're the seed for next year's bean crop. For a few years, I tried saving bean seeds that were especially colorful or had unusual fleck patterns in the hope of propagating some subtle mutation in the next generation. But as Mendel found with his peas, those details often disappear from one generation to the next.

ON OCTOBER 30, the US had just shy of a hundred thousand new cases in a single day, the newest record in a recent string of disheartening records.

NOVEMBER

EVEN THE TAMARACKS are confused now, unsure of what it's time to do. Over by the swale, several are at their autumnal best, a brilliant yolk-gold as explosive as their spring chartreuse. Others have started to shift from vivid gold to dusky ginger-orange, while one has dropped almost all its needles already. The two by the road still cling to their chlorophyll, lag the others by a week or more.

THE GARDEN IS nearly done for the season, with just carrots and some herbs left. I potted the rosemary plants, brought them inside for the winter. Some folks have great luck getting rosemary to overwinter; we don't. One of our cats adores the smell and flavor, and she nibbles the needly leaves and troubles the soil every chance she gets. Excluding the bedrooms and bathrooms, we have just one room with a door she can't open, so I keep the pots in there and hope.

TODAY IS ELECTION Day. According to exit polls, the main issues on voters' minds are the pandemic, the economy, and racial inequality. Rob and I voted by mail a couple weeks ago; the prospect of standing in a long, slow-moving line to vote in-person felt far too risky. All over the country, record numbers of people have voted already. Even so, the news is full of reports about long lines. People are waiting five, ten, even eleven hours to cast their ballots.

I'VE BEEN DEHYDRATING herbs for the last week, am doing sage right now. Each morning, I fill several circular, stackable trays with the soft, faintly furred leaves. Each tray is a plastic lattice, the spaces small enough that only tiny seeds or leaves can slip through; the stack of trays sits atop a heating unit I've set to 100 degrees, and a fan circulates warm air through the trays. Though an even hum, the dehydrator's drone is annoying, so I run it at night, far from our bedroom. Each morning, I gather curled and crackly leaves, pack them away to use through the winter, then harvest more fresh ones and refill the trays.

Drying herbs—albeit not with a powered dehydrator—is among the oldest and easiest preservation methods. Many kinds of herbs can be dried by making them into little posies and hanging them upside down in a well-ventilated space, like a barn or pass-through. When I've dried herbs this way, I put each posy in a big paper bag. The bag prevents them from getting dusty, and its size ensures the air will circulate around the leaves, reducing the chances they'll mold.

Lots of other foods can be dehydrated or air-dried, though the only ones I do are cherry tomatoes and apples. Fruits are good contenders for air-drying, especially berries and cherries and stone fruits. Carrots, beets, broccoli, and quite a few other vegetables, along with peanuts, sunflower seeds, pumpkin seeds and lean meats can all be preserved by careful air-drying.

BY THE TIME I woke up on Wednesday, the election results for most states had been called. Most, but not enough to know who won. On Thursday, Michigan and Wisconsin were called for Biden; Trump had had an early lead in both, but Biden edged past him once the absentee ballots were counted. On Friday, Arizona, Nevada, Georgia, North Carolina, and Pennsylvania were still counting. Shortly before noon on Saturday, more than three days after the polls closed, Pennsylvania was called in Biden's favor. That put him over the 270 electoral college votes needed to win, but President Trump isn't conceding. A few minutes after the Associated Press called Pennsylvania, Trump tweeted that Biden was "rushing to falsely pose as the winner." He is challenging the results not only in Pennsylvania, but also those in other close races.

AFTER I PUT away the most recent batch of sage leaves, I harvest some thyme to dehydrate. Unlike sage, thyme leaves are tiny, so I cut sections from the plant, half a dozen or so woody stems in each, and fill the trays with those. Tomorrow, when the leaves are dry and I rub them off, they'll turn into perfectly sized flakes.

I want to focus on these pleasant end-of-season tasks, but I'm fretting about the election. After prepping the thyme, I start googling other times a US presidential election didn't go smoothly. I remember Bush-Gore, the one that comes up first. After scrolling past lots of references to the recount and the eventual Supreme Court ruling for that election, I find a far older case, one I'd never known about, involving Thomas Jefferson.

THOMAS JEFFERSON AND John Adams, two of the Founding Fathers, were good friends during the lead-up to the Revolutionary War. However, after the war ended and the thirteen states were beginning to coalesce into a republic, the two men grew apart. Their fundamental disagreement concerned how much power the federal government should have and how much power should be retained by the individual states. Jefferson was a states' rights advocate who wanted limited federal control; Adams thought the newly formed republic needed more centralized power to make it cohere.

In 1796, Adams, who was vice president, ran against Jefferson, who was secretary of state, for the presidency. The race was ugly, and it further eroded the men's relationship. At that time, each member of the electoral college cast two votes; the candidate who got the most votes became president and the one with the second-most became vice president. Jefferson lost to Adams by just three votes, so he became a reluctant vice president to his frenemy from the rival party.

The two ran against each another again in 1800. To avoid any chance that rivals would have to serve together, each of the parties planned to have one elector throw a single vote. That way, the top-of-the-ticket candidate would beat his running mate by one vote, which would ensure they were elected as president and vice president, respectively. This time, Adams ran at the top of the Federalists' ticket, with Charles Pinckney as his running mate. Jefferson ran against him on the Democratic-Republican ticket, with Aaron Burr as running mate. In early December, the first of the electoral college votes reached Washington DC; within a few weeks, as the votes dribbled in, Adams realized he and Pinckney were going to lose. He wrote to a friend that he'd be returning to Massachusetts, where he would "potter in my garden among the fruit Trees and Cucumbers, and plant a Potatoe Yard with my own hand." When the electoral college votes were all tallied, Adams had sixty-five, Pinckney had sixty-four, and fellow Federalist John Jay had one.

But something went awry among the Democratic-Republican electors; rather than one of them throwing a vote so Jefferson would be the clear winner, Burr and Jefferson tied. The race went to the House of Representatives for them to decide. There, each state had one vote. In the first runoff, the two men tied again. As they did in the second. And third. And fourth. As they did, in fact, thirty-five times. Finally, on February 17, 1801, after the thirty-sixth round of voting, Thomas Jefferson was named president-elect. The election process was so fraught it prompted the creation of the Twelfth Amendment to replace the nation's original process for electing the president and vice president with a new one, the one we still use.

I'M TRYING TO decide which wait would have felt longer: three days in the twenty-first century, in the middle of a global pandemic, with news and fake news and social media cycles that run 24-7, or ten weeks in the early days of the nineteenth century when information moved at the speed of a rider on horseback.

EVENTUALLY, JEFFERSON AND Adams moved past their enmity and came to respect one another again. In their younger days, the two had shared a love of gardening, and both once again gardened avidly after their stints as president. In their zeal for growing plants, they were in good company. Many of the founders were enthusiasts. Benjamin Franklin sent home different kinds of turnips, cabbage, oats, barley, and beans from his postings abroad—and is credited with introducing rhubarb and Scotch kale to American farms and gardens. Though George Washington didn't introduce any novel plants to America's soil, he did ask sellers abroad to send him "the best kind" of their staple crops, and shared new wheat cultivars with fellow founder James Madison, among others.

The founders saved and exchanged seeds, read agricultural annals to keep apprised of new developments, and experimented with plant breeding. While their own botanical interests spanned the globe, the founders also thought small-scale farming was central to America's identity and to its citizens' well-being. For these statesmen, as Andrea Wulf observed in *Founding Gardeners*, "ploughing, planting and vegetable gardening were more than profitable and enjoyable occupations: they were also political acts, bringing freedom and independence."

While hardly the first to praise farmers for their natural nobility, America's founders did so as much to address their own fears and hopes as to express their faith that farmers would make the democratic experiment successful. The young country had just rejected Britain's authoritarian rule and was going to be governed by presidents and other elected officials who couldn't trace their authority back to a god, as Pharoah Hatshepsut did, couldn't point to a lineage of previous rulers whose mantles they were assuming, as Roman Emperors did. Lacking conventional proof of their right to govern, the leaders of the young republic needed to rally the citizenry around some common cause or vision to help the nation pull together and shore up their own power.

During the Revolutionary War, the shared concern was obvious. But afterward, John Adams feared there might not be "public Virtue enough to support a Republic." He thought the private virtues that farmers evinced could become the nation's public Virtue, an idea that Benjamin Franklin, George Washington, James Madison, and Thomas Jefferson agreed with. The founders regarded an abiding connection to the land, a strong work ethic, and a clear moral compass—all strengths they felt farmers cultivated—as the Virtues folks needed to establish a collective sense of themselves as Americans.

In 1794, in a letter, Washington wrote that he knew "of no pursuit in which more real and important services can be rendered to a country than by improving its agriculture." In *Notes on the State of Virginia*, Thomas Jefferson went further, writing "the greatest service which can be rendered any country is, to add an useful plant to its culture" and "cultivators of the earth are the most valuable citizens. They are the most vigorous, the most independent, the most virtuous, and they are tied to their country, and wedded to its liberty and interests by the most lasting bonds." He even argued that only farmers should be eligible for election to Congress because they are "the true representatives of the great American interest."

The leaders' emphasis on farming, both in their actions and their rhetoric, apparently paid off. Andrea Wulf wrote that when "the former colonies had to mature from being a war alliance to being a united nation . . . it was the Constitution that welded them together politically, legally and economically, but it was nature that provided a transcendent feeling of nationhood."

IF THEY REALLY had a transcendent feeling of nationhood, I envy them. We sure don't. Never in my lifetime has the country felt so divided. The only sentiments that seem widely shared are that the other side—whoever "the other" is—is gravely misguided and its poor judgment is ruining the nation. The exit polls on election night suggested we're evenly split in our enmity: 45 percent of voters said they would be "excited or optimistic" if Trump was re-elected, while 50 percent said they'd be "concerned or scared." Conversely, 50 percent said they'd be "excited or optimistic" if Biden was elected, while 46 percent said they'd be "concerned or scared."

PFIZER AND BIONTECH just announced the vaccine they're trialing is more than 90 percent effective in preventing COVID-19. *Ninety percent!* That's so much better than I dared hope. To get approval, vaccines only need a 50 percent efficacy rate. Experts have been bandying 60 percent as the likely rate for the first few vaccines. If this vaccine really is 90 percent effective, life might be more normal in a year or so. I'll get to see my mom in real life, get to go places safely, maybe even get to eat in a restaurant. It's oddly clarifying to realize what I most miss.

BETWEEN THE TEMPERATURE getting colder, the garden being mostly done for the year, and my unwise obsession with doomscrolling election news (on top of doomscrolling pandemic news), I haven't been spending much time outside. But the forecasters promise a high of 60 degrees today and I'm feeling more upbeat thanks to the Pfizer announcement, so I'm skipping the daily doomscroll. Rob and I are going to pick apples. We don't have to go far to do so: the few surviving trees from our intended orchard are all bearing fruit.

The forebears of those trees travelled halfway around the world to get to Maine, a place now well-known for its apples. Their journey began in Central Asia, where wild apples were domesticated somewhere between four thousand and ten thousand years ago. There, the trees were part of fruit forests, and grew among pomegranates, figs, apricots, pears, and cherries. Early apples were small, no bigger than a grape. While similar in size, the apples would have been wildly distinct from one another in most other ways because apple seeds, like potato seeds, contain tremendous genetic variability. Neither apple trees nor their fruit will necessarily look or taste like their parents.

Despite the apples' high genetic variability, bears in the region managed to impact the fruit's evolutionary trajectory. The bears preferred larger, sweeter apples to small ones, so more seeds from bigger apples ended up in their scat. The next generation of trees wouldn't necessarily bear large, sweet fruit, but they had the genes to do so, so their progeny might. Likewise, apples were carried west by humans travelling the Silk Roads. Traders undoubtedly seeded accidental orchards in their caravan-wakes.

Because apple seeds don't grow true, growers who want to make sure new trees maintain the parent's attributes graft a branch from the parent onto some hardy stock. Historians don't know exactly when or where grafting was invented, but they know grape growers in the Tigris Valley were doing it by the second millennium BCE. When Alexander the Great returned from the Tigris Valley to Greece, he reputedly carried both grafting knowledge and some dwarf apple trees with him. And Theophrastus (Aristotle's student who asked Alexander to bring him novel plants) wrote about various grafting techniques. As the Roman Empire expanded, soldiers and their contingents carried both apples and grafting knowledge with them.

Indeed, Michael Pollan notes that apple trees "followed the westward course of empire," reaching North America when European colonists came bearing Old World scions that they hoped to graft onto New World trees. Few of those efforts succeeded, so colonists resorted to growing trees from seed. Little of the fresh fruit was palatable, though that didn't overly trouble growers, who mostly wanted the apples to make hard cider.

WHEN I WAS planning our orchard, I chose twenty different cultivars, divided among four general categories: those whose fruits were good for fresh eating, for storing, for cooking, and for making cider. When the skinny whips arrived, I carefully noted where we planted each type. But by the time most of the trees had died, I could see that some of the survivors were not as advertised. So, I brought some apples with me when we went to the Common Ground Country Fair that year. As he does nearly every year, the apple expert John Bunker was spending an afternoon there looking at people's fruit samples and chatting about heirloom apples. The line to talk with him was long, so he limited folks to questions about just one apple each. Turns out the one I thought was a McIntosh was a Liberty. I'm still unsure about a couple trees, but feel more resigned now in my apple uncertainty, more comfortable letting flavor determine how we consume them.

When it comes to eating fresh apples, Rob and I have different tastes. His go-to apple in a market is the Granny Smith, and he likes the lone green apple we grow well enough. I think, and hope, it's a Rhode Island Greening. My store pick is Macoun, so it's no surprise I'm also a fan of the Liberty, which was created by crossing a Macoun with a Purdue 54-12. Macoun, in turn, is a cross between McIntosh and Jersey Black. I mistook the granddaughter, Liberty, for her grandmother, McIntosh.

Both Macoun and Liberty were developed at the Agricultural Experiment Station in Geneva, New York. Researchers there benefit enormously from being just a few doors down from one of the USDA's agricultural research facilities. That facility maintains collections of genetic material for brassicas, grapes, hemp, and squashes, among other species. But what it's best known for is its collection of apple germ; with over six thousand distinct accessions, it's one of the largest and most diverse apple collections in the world.

The USDA also maintains a large apple orchard there, where they grow two each of twenty-five hundred different varieties, a Noah's ark of apples. Michael Pollan toured the orchard as part of his research for *The Botany of Desire*. In it, he describes two rows of weirdly wonderful trees that were planted six years prior to his visit. The seeds for those trees had been gathered in Kazakhstani forests, where apples retain their "ineluctable wildness." Of the Kazakhstani trees, Pollan wrote that no two "looked even remotely alike, not in form or leaf or fruit. Some grew straight for the sun, others trailed along the ground or formed low shrubs or simply petered out, the up-state New York climate not to their liking. I saw apples with leaves like those of linden trees, others shaped like demented forsythia bushes." The apples themselves "looked and tasted like God's first drafts of what an apple could be."

Having grown up in north central Massachusetts, I've seen my fair share of apple orchards, scrambled up plenty of semi-dwarf trees, and tasted many, many drops. But after reading Pollan's description of the Kazakhstani trees, I longed to see the USDA orchard. I imagined that walking the long rows, moving from the ur-apples to the domesticated ones, would be like walking through time, that I could witness the apples evolving as the genetic plenitude of *Malus sieversii* gradually gave way to the several thousand distinct *M. domestica*.

A few years after Pollan's book came out, I had the chance to visit those trees. Rather than moving from past to present, walking the evolutionary route, my actual path carried me backward through time. The first trees I encountered had been recently planted, still so young they were tethered to metal poles to help them stay upright until their trunks were thicker and stronger. I hurried past them in search of something stranger. As I got farther into the orchard, the trees grew taller—though seldom tall—and their crowns larger. Though not heavily pruned the way most orchards are, these trees were familiar. Their leaves were recognizably apple-y and their boughs held fruit that was, for the most part, recognizably apple-y or crab apple-y. But the array of fruit hues was amazing: pale yellow, deep banana yellow, sundry greens, brilliant crimsons, pinky reds, dusky purples and, on the ground, every shade of brown as rotting fruit gradually returned to earth.

At last I reached a much more densely green space—the wild rows. The air was soupy with sweetness and rot, thick with insects. The ground was carpeted with fruits ranging from tiny crab apple-sized clusters to softball-sized globes.

Some looked like cherries, others like arctic kiwis. Some were heavily pocked, some scabby, some stippled, some mottled, some smooth. Some were dusky, others as shiny as a supermarket sample. Forewarned, I tasted just a few; they were so puckeringly tart I felt like I had a mouthful of chalk. Cider apples seem sweet by comparison.

NONE OF THE apples in our yard have the same degree of genetic variety that those old ones do. They are heirlooms, yes, but they mostly date back to the 1800s and 1900s. The Rhode Island Greening, if it is one, is the oldest, a cultivar dating back to 1650. Our tree doesn't bear much fruit, and its apples are the first to fall. We gathered just three from it today. But the other trees still held so many ripe apples that Rob and I quickly filled a ten-gallon garden trug. My plan is to turn this haul into applesauce and a nonalcoholic cider. When I'm done dehydrating the rest of the herbs, I'll make apple chips.

We don't have a fruit press, but it's possible to make cider using just extra-fine cheesecloth and a couple of large stock pots, ideally in the sixteen-to-twenty-quart range. Even though I know they haven't been sprayed, I start by washing the apples. Then, without peeling or coring them, I cut the apples into quarters, tossing them into the pot until it's about four inches shy of full. For flavoring, I use several cinnamon sticks, some whole cloves and whole nutmegs, and a cup of brown sugar. Then, I add enough water to more than cover the apples. Once it comes to a boil, I turn the heat down to simmer, cover the pot, and let it be for a few hours. When the apples are mushy, I mash them and then let the whole thing simmer for another hour, this time without a cover so some of the liquid evaporates away.

While the apple mush simmers, I line the other pot with cheesecloth, making sure that plenty of it hangs out over the sides. Then, I transfer the mush onto the cheesecloth, gradually lifting the cloth up and gathering the edges together to form a pouch. Most of the liquid seeps through the cheesecloth right away and settles in the pot. By this point, the cheesecloth pouch contains the semi-solid bits of apple and spices. I tie it into a sack and put an extra-long wooden spoon through the knot, as if it were a bindle. The wooden spoon is long enough to rest on the edges of the pot, and it holds the apple mush above the liquid cider. More cider will drip from the bindle into the pot over the next couple hours. This simple process generates far more cider than we can drink in a few days, so we store the extra in freezer bags in the deep freeze, take out a quart or two as we need it.

AFTER SURGING LAST spring, the number of COVID-19 cases in Maine trended downward from June until the end of October. Then, as if marking the change of seasons, that trend ended early this month. Cases numbers throughout the state are climbing quickly now, as are hospital and ICU admissions.

Last week, everyone on our COVID-19 task force call was giddy with relief about the possibility of an effective vaccine; this week, everyone's somber again. *Nature* released a study on the eleventh that's getting a lot of news coverage. It says indoor public places—especially restaurants and grocery stores and gyms—are where people are becoming infected most often. Though not surprising, it's disheartening—especially to Wayne, who is a pastor and wants to be able to hold church services in person, and to Mike, the superintendent for our school.

Everyone on the task force knows we aren't done, but right now, it's hard to know what we need to—or should—do next. After many months of uncertainty, changing information, and other updates, the advice from the CDC has become consistent and stable, so we aren't putting out fliers or updating the website pages anymore. And with tourists and summer folks gone, we no longer need to prepare lists of local resources and addresses for organizations offering COVID tests. We can urge year-round folks to stay safe during the holidays, amplify the CDC's recommendations, but people's attitudes are increasingly fixed, unlikely to be changed even by well-meaning friends and neighbors.

ON NOVEMBER 16, Moderna announced that its experimental vaccine works, and that it has a 94.5 percent efficacy rate, which is astonishing. They, too, are applying for emergency use authorization. We may have not one, but two, extremely good vaccines by the beginning of next year.

VACCINES USUALLY CONTAIN the virus they are meant to protect against. Sometimes the virus is dead; sometimes it's alive but has been made much weaker. When it enters the body, the immune system knows it's foreign and begins to mount a defense, which is why many folks feel a little sick after they get vaccinated. Having learned how to fight against a dead or weak version of the virus, the immune system can immediately mount a defense if it's exposed to the real thing.

These new vaccines work differently. Instead of using a dead virus, the vaccines use a strand of its RNA, a piece of viral genetic code that was sequenced in a lab. In both new vaccines, the RNA codes for a protein in one of the spikes sticking out from the virus. When the vaccine enters the body, the immune system recognizes the RNA as foreign, and the body begins to develop a response to fight against it. Since the vaccine gives the immune system a preview of the spike's structure, it learns how to make an antibody to attach to it and stop it from entering cells. Later, if the body is exposed to the actual coronavirus, it will be able to make antibodies immediately. Of course, neither of these vaccines can stop the coronavirus from entering a body, but if they are as good as the manufacturers say, then they should significantly reduce how sick people get if it does. And because the vaccines don't include the genes for the whole virus, people who get a shot won't get even a mild case of COVID-19.

SINCE THE VACCINES are at least several months from being available, the CDC is urging people not to gather for Thanksgiving. Rob and I have never had a Thanksgiving alone. In graduate school, we were part of a big friend group that celebrated it together. After that, we always celebrated with my family. When Rob and I hosted, we'd start prepping Wednesday morning. Even before the first guests arrived that evening, I'd have made cranberry sauce and a pie or two. Rob would have filled a huge bag with brine and started the turkey soaking in it. We loved turning the meal into a two-day family gathering, with crocks of soup simmering on the stove for folks who got in Wednesday night, a fire in the woodstove, music.

YESTERDAY, WHEN I went out to the chest freezer to disinter some cider, I found six pieces of baklava. Early in the pandemic, when we were searching for something different to do, we took a Zoom cooking class about Greek food in which we learned to make fake souvlaki and real baklava. Since it's just the two of us for Thanksgiving dinner, I took out the baklava, figuring we could have that for dessert instead of pie.

This morning, I tore a small loaf of bread into chunks for the stuffing, chopped the celery and onions. It was so quiet I put on the radio to drown out the missing voices. Instead of a turkey, we got a chicken from Grace Pond Farm. We'll have potatoes and carrots from the garden, cranberry sauce, and stuffing.

When everything is ready, I light candles, even though it is midafternoon and still light.

In lieu of a traditional prayer, we usually go around the table on Thanksgiving, and everyone says what they're most grateful for that year. I try, stumble.

"I'm sorry," I say, as my eyes fill with tears. "I should have made a pie."

Rob shakes his head. "We don't need one."

"And the stuffing's too bready. I didn't know how to make just a little."

"No," he reaches for my hand. "It's fine. I swear."

He's right. Though the stuffing is not the best, I'm sure we'll eat it over the next day or two. But in this moment, bowed by the weight of all that's missing, neither of us can savor our dinner. The absences feel so freighted, as if each is itself and a token of all that's been lost this year.

AFTER MY DAD died, I began having dreams in which he didn't undergo heart surgery, and therefore didn't suffer a stroke midsurgery, and therefore didn't begin so soon on the path of inexorable decline. Instead, he's in decent health, and we inhabit a well-delineated alternative timeline. I love spending time there. But doing so comes with a string attached, one thick as a mooring line: no one can acknowledge it, can't so much as hint at how amazing it is, how lucky we are to get this unlikely do-over. If anyone does, our miracle will turn into an ordinary dream.

DECEMBER

❦ ❦

THE YARD, LIKE the landscape more generally, is at its most monochrome now. All the garden plants and weeds have died back. We've cleaned up most of the beds, done an okay job getting them ready for winter. I always intend to do a great job, as I know it'll pay off the next spring. But end-of-season tasks aren't much fun, and I'm mentally ready to be done. The greenhouse is full of pots and plant supports and lawn chairs. Through the clear panes, I can see the fabric grow bags piled on the long counter—orange and purple and deep royal blue. They're the only bits of bright color we'll have in the yard until next spring.

The lawn is dun, and the shrubs and trees have shed their leaves for winter, the tamaracks included. Unlike most conifers, tamarack shed all their needles annually, making them easy to spot among the actual evergreens. They look spindly and frail compared to the spruces and firs, but their lack of needles can be a boon during winter storms. Snow wafts through naked branches more readily than through their needled counterparts, so tamarack boughs are less likely to break under the weight of wet snow. Spruces and firs have also evolved strategies for shedding snow: their branches are shorter toward the top, so the skinniest don't hold as much snow; and the branches are flexible, so they don't inevitably snap under a snow-load. Whether one of those evolutionary strategies is better than the other probably depends on local conditions.

A NEW, MORE transmissible variant of the coronavirus is gaining traction. It's not yet clear whether people are becoming sicker or if they're getting long COVID more often. What is clear is that a lot more people are getting sick. Maine is reporting new record numbers of cases and hospitalizations almost every day. Nearly two-hundred thousand people in the US and more than six-hundred thousand people worldwide are testing positive daily.

Public health people assumed this would happen. If a beneficial mutation gives a certain version of the virus a big advantage, then that version is nearly guaranteed dominance, which is one of the reasons pandemics so often happen in waves. Though I expected variants would appear, I kept hoping we could escape the emergence of a superbug.

OUR FRIEND MARK is part of a group called the Positive Deviance Collaborative, a cohort of consultants and researchers and change agents who work to address significant social problems worldwide. Their method is straightforward, but not simplistic. They note that in every community, a minority—

often a tiny minority—of people find much better solutions to tough problems than do the other community members, and that they find those solutions without more or better resources than everyone else. Those problem solvers deviate from the norm, but in a positive way, hence the group's name.

When members of the Positive Deviance Collaborative are asked to come help solve a problem, they don't bring prepackaged proposals. Instead, they look for these outliers, the people in the community who've figured out how to solve the problem well. Then, they see if adopting a similar approach could work for the many. If so, everyone in the community can, potentially, have better nutrition, or greater early childhood health, or greater safety for women, for example. Instead of focusing on what's going wrong and trying to fix that, Positive Deviance focuses on what's going right and encouraging more of the same.

To mark the collaborative's thirtieth anniversary, members were gathering for a day-long Zoom meeting/celebration. Knowing I'm fascinated by their approach, Mark invited me to attend. Members talked about some of their most momentous projects, including their very first, which began in 1991 and focused on childhood malnutrition in Vietnam. There, they discovered some parents augmented the typical diet for children with tiny shrimps and crabs that lived in the rice paddies and with sweet potato greens. Modest though those additions sound, the extra protein and nutrients made a big difference in their children's health. Throughout the 1990s, the Positive Deviance consultants helped to elevate approaches that similarly centered Indigenous food knowledge, and those practices helped more than two million people in 250 Vietnamese communities. Actually, I bet it's benefitted many more, since people probably didn't stop adding shellfish and greens to their diets just because the consultants stopped tracking what was happening.

Despite having learned a lot about the approach from Mark, I was astounded. He and his colleagues have helped literally tens of millions of people better their life circumstances—not by telling them what to do, but by helping them see what a neighbor has been doing all along.

NOT WANTING TO chance people getting sick, the town manager cancelled both Santa's annual fire-truck ride through town and the Christmas tree lighting ceremony at the town office. I feel relieved that, at last, he's publicly taking steps to protect folks. People understood the need to cancel, but so many expressed disappointment that the local Santa's real-life wife suggested we organize a town-wide holiday-lights event instead. People could decorate their outdoor spaces and then, on a weekend close to Christmas, everyone could drive around, admire the displays, and vote for their favorites.

Rob and I live on a dead-end street with just a handful of winter residents. Normally, we don't put up outdoor decorations. But I got corralled into making the map of participating houses and businesses—which made me feel like we should put up a few lights at least. An afternoon of online hunting later, I'd located solar-powered strings of star-shaped lights that, miraculously, were not on back order. I bought four. They arrived a few days later and we looped them around a shapely spruce near the end of the driveway. To illuminate its peak, Rob perched on the top step of a ladder and flung the end of the last string of lights, which caught on the highest branch.

Once the batteries had gathered enough energy to turn the lights on, we went back outside to see how the tree looked. The lights blinked on and off in what might have been a lovely, twinkly effect if only the on-ing and off-ing of the bulbs on each string were staggered. But they weren't. Instead, when the lights on one string turned off, they all turned off, leaving a section of the spruce dark. When that string came back on, another entire string turned off, miring a different section in darkness.

WE'RE IN THE darkest time of the year. Today we had only nine hours of light. For more than a week surrounding winter solstice, we'll be down to eight hours and fifty-two minutes each day. At Christmas, the days will begin to lengthen again, though I usually can't perceive the change until mid-January. On summer solstice, we have nearly twice as much daylight as on its winter counterpart, fifteen hours and thirty minutes on that longest day.

Those lengthy days are why we grow "long-day onions," why potatoes do so well here. Why we endure the difficult darkness now.

IN THE GARDEN, only the carrots remain. When my nieces and nephews were young and I was hoping to broaden their interest in vegetables, I grew a rainbow of carrots—white, yellow, orange, red, and purple. Lately, I grow just one or two orange cultivars, usually Yayas or Boleros.

The carrots' leaves have been nibbled off; just nubby hints of their weathered stalks remain. Some of the carrots' greenish-orangy shoulders have pushed up above the soil line, and I can see that they've been gnawed. But for the most part, the carrots are safely underground. I've left them in this long because being exposed to the cold makes them sweeter. When live carrots get very cold, they convert some of the starch stored in their roots into sugar, which mingles with the water in their cells. Sugar water freezes at a lower temperature than plain old water, so the cells don't burst. The carrots become intensely sweet.

Once the temperature drops, I game the weather forecasts. I want to wait for maximum sugar. But if I wait too long, the ground will be frozen solid. Even if the carrots are intact when I dig them out, their sugar-water strategy won't have been enough. They'll crumble or turn to mush as soon as they thaw.

WHILE I WAIT for a propitious day to harvest the carrots, I hole up in my study for several afternoons, learning more about the plant's history. Turns out that scholars know less about the domestication of carrots than about many other important foods, in part because early commentators used the same words for carrots and parsnips. They do know that wild carrots likely originated in what is now Afghanistan, where they were considered more medicinal than culinary. When those carrots reached Greece, they were widely crossed with local versions. According to Plutarch, even the crossed carrots had a bitter flavor and a fiery nature, an assessment much like that of physician Galen, who was the first, at least among Western writers, to clearly distinguish between carrots and parsnips. According to his humoral theory, carrots were a warming and drying food, one that promoted the production of yellow bile. He believed they could help alleviate flatulence by encouraging farting. As it happens, consuming a lot of carrots causes both flatulence and farting—which would (presumably) diminish the aphrodisiacal effects the ancient Greeks also ascribed to them.

THE PURPLE CARROTS I've grown were Cosmic Purple and Purple Haze, names that led me to think of them as recent additions to the carrot world. And while those specific cultivars probably were, their anthocyanin-rich forebears date back millennia. The earliest domesticated carrots were purple and yellow; carrots of both colors were grown throughout Europe for several centuries. By the 1500s, yellow carrots were significantly more popular. Orange carrots are believed to have originated due to a mutation in yellow carrots that was then selected for. Dutch farmers working during the late 1500s are often credited with that breeding effort. It's quite possible, though, that orange carrots arrived earlier than that. The English word "orange" wasn't used to describe a color until 1512. Instead, people described what we think of as orange as *ġeolurēad*, yellow-red; so some carrots referred to as yellowish-red or reddish-yellow prior to 1512 might have been orange.

I suspect orange carrots were becoming relatively common before the Dutch focused on breeding them. Earlier this year, when I was searching for the stories of my heirloom melons, I found several paintings of melon amid the fruits and vegetables in the festoons the Renaissance painter Giovanni Martini da Udine painted in the loggia of the Villa Farnesina in 1518. Da Udine also painted at least one purple carrot and one orange carrot in the festoons. And while I'm still hesitant about saying one of the melons in the painting is definitely the same cultivar as my Italian heirloom, I'm quite confident in saying the orange carrot in Da Udine's festoon is orange.

Even if the Dutch weren't responsible for developing the first orange carrots, they were at the forefront of carrot breeding in general. During the 1500s, they cultivated and stabilized four carrot types—the Early Long, Late Half Long, Scarlet Horn, and Long Orange. These four are the antecedents of all the orange hybrids grown today.

By the end of that century, carrots were so popular in England that the author of a gardening how-to book urged people there to grow their own, rather than paying for imported produce. He complained that a "great aboundance of carrets are brought by forraine nations to this land, whereby they have received yéerely great summes of mony and commodities out of this land." And he pointed out that carrots are quite versatile; they can be "boyled," eaten raw, or used in "dainty sallets." They're also healthful, able to "give good nourishment to all people, are not hurtfull to any, whatsoever infirmities they be diseased of." He concluded by exhorting his country people to "sowe Carrets in your Gardens, and humbly praise God for them, as for a singuler and great blessing."

As did apples, domesticated carrots followed the course of empire. They were introduced into Mexico by the Spanish and into North America by English colonists. Like many other crops brought over by English settlers, carrots grew especially well in the northern and mid-Atlantic regions and became a popular choice for kitchen gardens. Thomas Jefferson grew several varieties at Monticello, with the goal of harvesting at least three bushels per year. While he specifically noted that he planted *carote di Pisa* (carrots from Pisa) in 1774, Jefferson usually just logged that he'd planted "carrots." Only occasionally did he add anything more particular, like that they were "early red" or "large red" or "orange."

The seeds for a carrot called Rouge Demi-Longue de Chantenay, a short orange carrot with a red core, are included in the Thomas Jefferson Center for Historic Plants, a repository and nursery at Monticello dedicated to maintaining historic seeds. Jefferson himself almost certainly did not grow Rouge Demi-Longues, but the center stocks the seeds because they were an important cultivar during the nineteenth century. When Michelle Obama established a White House Garden nearly two centuries later, it included Rouge Demi-Longue de Chantenay and several other plants from Monticello to commemorate Thomas Jefferson and his gardening legacy.

Like other Founding Fathers, Jefferson experimented with plants and encouraged others to do the same. He praised the burgeoning agricultural societies whose members were trying new crops and reporting on their efforts. "In an infant country, as ours is, these experiments are important," Jefferson wrote, adding that of course not all the experiments would succeed:

finding new crops "will require abundance of unsuccessful ex-periments. But if, in a multitude of these, we make one useful acquisition, it repays our trouble."

Many federal officials in the nineteenth century imbued not only domestic policies but also foreign relations with their passions for plants. In 1819, the secretary of the treasury asked naval officers and ambassadors to gather seeds from foreign re-gions and send them home because "the introduction of use-ful plants, not before cultivated, or of such as are of superior quality to those which have been previously introduced, is an object of great importance to every civilized state." He assured officials that "the collectors of the different ports of the United States will cheerfully cooperate with you in this interesting and beneficent undertaking."

Similarly, during his presidency, John Quincy Adams urged naval officers to gather plants materials to create "the nucleus" of the national botanic garden. Like the ancient Egyptians, Greeks, Romans, and others, the United Sates was relying on its military to scout out novel plants. But compared to other mod-ern nations, the US was late to the plant-hunting game. Euro-pean nations were already sending botanists abroad on military ships and other expeditions.

One especially important international plant accession occurred in 1851, when an American consul stationed in Cen-tral America sent potatoes from Panama back to the United States. He directed them to Reverend Chauncey Goodrich, who'd become an avid potato breeder in the wake of the Great Potato Famine in Ireland in the 1840s. When he received the Panamanian potatoes, Goodrich crossed them with commercially available potatoes to improve the vigor of the latter. He hoped the new cultivars would be able to withstand exposure to late blight and other diseases. His work paid off; while potatoes are still susceptible to blight, almost all potato varieties now available in the US are descendants of those crosses, and many are resistant to scab, mosaic viruses, wilt, and other potato diseases.

CONGRESS AUTHORIZED ESTABLISHING the Agricultural Division of the Patent Office and made it responsible not only for gathering new seed, but also for distributing it to farmers—for free. By 1850, more than eighty thousand packets of seed were distributed annually through its auspices. The government hoped farmers would find cultivars well-suited to conditions in their regions and would pursue on-farm breeding programs to develop even better strains.

As the nation and its farm programs grew, farmers—and many federal officials—thought agriculture needed its own department. In 1862, Congress established an independent Department of Agriculture and moved the seed program from the Patent Office to it. The free seed program grew rapidly: in 1888, more than 4.6 million seed packets were distributed. In truth, that growth wasn't entirely beneficial. Many farmers complained they received ordinary seed, not new cultivars. And quite a bit of seed went not to farmers, but to home gardeners and others. Still, the program achieved its goals overall. New crops entered the mix and productive cultivars were fine-tuned through on-farm breeding efforts.

As farmers saved the best of their seed, they developed varieties suited to their locales, climates, weather conditions. Farmers growing green beans in New England, for example, may have saved seed for the plants that matured the most quickly, while those in the mid-Atlantic might have selected for a longer, thinner bean, and farmers in the South for plants with the best heat tolerance. Even if all these farmers began with seed from the same batch, the seed each saved soon diverged from the rest, became a little less like that saved by farmers in other regions or farmers with other priorities. Selecting for the traits they valued, the farmers were altering the plants' germ lines. While all the beans were still *P. vulgaris*, they were no longer alike.

I wonder what this can teach us about transformation, about how something becomes something else. How—and how much—can a thing change and still be itself? How—or how much—must a thing change before it ceases to be its old self?

THE ELECTORAL COLLEGE members have cast their votes; Joe Biden is on his way to being president-elect. Donald Trump continues to insist he won, says the election was marred by widespread fraud. A few hours after the electoral college finished its vote count, Biden said, "In this battle for the soul of America, democracy prevailed. We the people voted, faith in our institutions held, the integrity of our elections remains intact."

But did it? Did faith in our institutions really hold? Did the integrity of our elections really remain intact? And if they didn't, did democracy prevail? Is it battered, but still itself? Or is democracy mutating, evolving before our eyes?

WITH THE GARDEN done for the year, I've been leaning hard on poetry for sustenance. In last week's *New Yorker*, Brenda Hillman had a gorgeous short poem called "Winter Song for One Who Suffers." It feels so apt to this moment that I copied out a few lines and taped them on a wall so I can read them when I need to: "A soul can crouch / a long time while the heart / expands to reach its edges."

Yes, it can.

THE FOOD AND Drug Administration just issued emergency use authorization to Pfizer-BioNTech for their vaccine. That news makes *my* heart expand.

THE LIGHT UP St. George decoration extravaganza was this past weekend. Saturday, the weather was truly miserable, raining hard all day and well into the night. I didn't see many cars drive by. But Sunday was clear and dry; cars streamed down the street, many of them honking at each other. One was decorated with holiday lights that flashed on and off in the appropriate, twinkly way. Quite reasonably, no one selected our sad display as a favorite. In fact, no one has even mentioned seeing it. But since the lights are up, we figure we might as well leave them until after Christmas.

Maybe they'll deter the deer.

Our local COVID-19 task force is having its last meeting before taking a hiatus until after New Year's. Everyone is in high spirits on the Zoom call. After some general and generally jubilant chatter, Kate takes conversational point. She's familiar with the issues that arise during the rollout of a novel vaccine and is telling the rest of us what to expect and where we should focus.

Getting the vaccine is probably a ways off since our town doesn't have any hospitals or clinics, any drug stores, any doctor's or nurse's offices. So, during the several months before it's widely available, she urges us to focus on reducing vaccine hesitancy and increasing vaccine equity in the community. Along with folks' personal physicians, she says, peers and pastors tend to be the most trusted information sources in situations like this. She encourages everyone to get vaccinated the moment they're eligible and to talk about it matter-of-factly, as if it's the most ordinary thing in the world.

Doctors and medical researchers don't know what percentage of people need to be immune to COVID-19 before we achieve herd immunity, but it's likely high. For a while, I'd assumed we could reach herd immunity within six months, a year tops, once a vaccine was available, since vaccinated people's immunity would be combined with the immunity of those who have had COVID. But more and more people are getting infected multiple times. The rise in the reinfection rate means folks can't be sure how long—or even if—they'll remain immune. Likewise, we don't know how long the immunity from the vaccines will last.

EULA BISS WROTE about herd immunity in her book *On Immunity: An Inoculation*. She pointed out that herd immunity allows the collective body to achieve a level of protection some individual bodies can't attain on their own: "An unvaccinated person is protected by the bodies around her, bodies through which disease is not circulating. But a vaccinated person surrounded by bodies that host disease is left vulnerable to vaccine failure or fading immunity." In this sense, herd immunity is a gift, a way of spreading the health of the hale to the frail. The immunity—or lack thereof—of those around us led Biss to observe that "we are protected not so much by our own skin, but by what is beyond it. The boundaries between our bodies begin to dissolve here." I love this way of framing the fact that we are all connected, that what each one does will influence the whole.

When I envision those dissolving body boundaries, I don't channel low-res horror movies or medical documentaries. Instead, I picture the photogram portraits the artist Christopher Bucklow began making in the 1990s. Like old-fashioned silhouettes, they are often person-shaped. Whereas the inside of the figure in a silhouette is typically solid and dark, Bucklow uses the sun to fill these contours with thousands of points of light, depicting the subject as radiant, pure energy. Even the areas around the figures glow, aura-like. In photograms that depict pairs of people, the dot density doubles in the places where the figures overlap, as if what once belonged to each has become part of both—like the many viruses we can't live without, the seeds with whom we've become utterly entangled, the resistance or immunity we can share with one another.

THIS MORNING, I went to the post office in our village to mail a few holiday packages. It's very small; the space for customers is no more than eight feet deep by eighteen wide, maybe less. On the door is an official sign from the USPS stating that masks are required inside. But behind his plexiglass shield, the postmaster was mask-less—as were the two customers ahead of me.

I went outside to wait. The parking lot for the post office is so small I'd had to park across the street at the Baptist church, which was good because I didn't have to talk to the other customers when they came out. I wanted to avoid the confrontation that could arise if either was an emphatic mask-opponent. While I embrace, even cherish, the idea that all beings are interconnected, the ordinary reality of that can be challenging to navigate when you live in a small town.

After both customers drove away, I went back in, bought postage for the packages, and checked my PO Box. In the furled mishmash of mail was the first seed catalog of the season. It's so fat it has a perfect binding instead of a stapled one. Though it's dedicated to heirloom seeds, there's a teaser promising dozens of great "new" varieties, by which the writers mean a medley of old varieties that are once again available and seeds from abroad that have recently been approved for sale in the US.

As soon as I'm home, I toss the other mail aside and start to skim the catalog, more than ready to envision a new year full of possibilities.

AFTERWORD

A ND JUST LIKE that, after the year that lasted at least a decade, two more have passed at a more familiar pace. As if on schedule, a succession of SARS-CoV-2 variants emerged, generating waves of disease that undulated around the globe, apparently our new (ab)normal. Even areas spared early on suffered during these successive outbreaks. Political and social divisions continue to exacerbate public health emergencies—not just COVID-19, but also those caused by climate disruptions. Massive wildfires, glacial melt, warming oceans, prolonged droughts, mammoth rainfalls, and record-breaking temperatures are all increasingly common.

Accepting that COVID-19 will be endemic, the United States plans to have vaccines available annually, much like flu shots. Schools are open and now have few, if any, disease-related restrictions. Businesses whose employees were able to work remotely are urging them to come back to the office. Some supply chain woes persist, but as far as I know, hand sanitizer and toilet paper are no longer being hoarded.

And here? Saint George was not magically spared, of course. But living at the end of the earth does reduce one's exposure to all novelties, including novel germs. The task force disbanded in April 2021, no longer needed. With my wimpy immune system bolstered by two shots of the initial vaccine and two boosters, I go out into the world without the wracking terror of early 2020 or the roller coaster of emotions that dominated autumn. But I still spend lots of time in our yard, more contentedly now that the tree line no longer marks the edge of my world. The garden isn't getting as much attention as it did in 2020, but I try to stay ahead of the weeds (mostly) and feed the needy plants. And, in return, they continue to nourish our bodies and hearts.

NOTES

MARCH

Page 6, *"Having a name matters"*: WHO Director-General's remarks at the media briefing on 2019-nCoV on 11 February 2020, available at https://www.who.int/dg/speeches/detail/who-director-general-s-remarks-at-the-media-briefing-on-2019-ncov-on-11-february-2020.

Page 6, *A few days later, Ghebreyesus called on social media companies*: WHO Director General's Speech at the Munich Security Conference, 15 February 2020. Available at https://www.who.int/director-general/speeches/detail/munich-security-conference

Page 7, *They hoped to see COVID-19 "spontaneously petering out"*: A. Lee, "Wuhan Novel Coronavirus (COVID-19): why global control is challenging?" National Library of Medicine. Available at https://www.ncbi.nlm.nih.gov/pmc/articles/PMC7130979/

Page 11, *"When you start a garden"*: Dan Barber, "You Say Tomato, I say Agricultural Disaster," *New York Times*, August 8, 2009.

Page 12, *The philosopher Hannah Arendt*: Quoted in Ilya Winham, "Rereading Hannah Arendt's 'What is Freedom?: Freedom as a Phenomenon of Political Virtuosity," *Theoria: A Journal of Social and Political Theory* (June 2012), Vol 59, No. 131, pp. 84-106, p. 91.

Page 17, *I told my friend*: David McCullough, Commencement Address at Wesleyan College, June 1984.

Page 20, *Remains there reveal that the sedentary hunter-gatherers*: Thor Hanson, *The Triumph of Seeds: How Grains, Nuts, Kernels, Pulses & Pips Conquered the Plant Kingdom and Shaped Human History*. New York: Basic Books, 2015. p. 28.

Page 21, *According to the biologist*: Jonathan Silvertown, *An Orchard Invisible: A Natural History of Seeds*. Chicago: University of Chicago Press, 2009, p. 148.

Page 21, *Instead of eating many different foods*: Hanson, 28.

Page 24, *And it tastes great*: Anson Mills, "Rustic Red Fife Bread Flour." Available at https://anson-mills.myshopify.com/collections/retail-products/products/rustic-red-fife-bread-flour.

Page 26, *It certainly served her well*: Kara Cooney, *The Woman who would be King*. New York: Broadway Books, 2014, p. 73.

Page 26, *If the gods were pleased*: Cooney, p. 16.

Page 27, *A relief in Hatshepsut's temple*: F. D. P. Wicker, "The Road to Punt," *The Geographical Journal*, Vol. 164, No. 2 (July 1998), pp. 155–67, pp. 163–4.

Page 27, *Text accompanying another image*: D. M. Dixon, "The Transplantation of Punt Incense Trees in Egypt," *The Journal of Egyptian Archaeology*, Vol. 55 (Aug. 1969), pp. 55–65, p. 60.

Page 27, *One Egyptologist proposed*: Dixon, p. 64.

APRIL

Page 31, *The anthropologist Richard Wrangham believes*: Bridget Alex, "Humans Domesticated Dogs and Cows. We May Have Also Domesticated Ourselves." *Discover Magazine* (May 3, 2019). Available at https://www.discovermagazine.com/planet-earth/humans-domesticated-dogs-and-cows-we-may-have-also-domesticated-ourselves.

Page 37, *In fact, they were so loved*: U. P. Hedrick, *Sturtevant's notes on edible plants*. Albany, NY: J. B. Lyon Company, 1919, p. 203.

Page 38, *All the same, the frescoes in the villa*: Jules Janick, "Fruits and Nuts of the Villa Farnesina." *Arnoldia*, Vol 70, No. 2 (2012), pp. 20–27.

Page 41, *The pope knew King Charles had been entranced*: Gillian Mawrey, "Garden Review: Chateau Gaillard, Amboise, France," *Historic Gardens Review*, No. 35 (February 2017), pp. 34–36, p. 34.

Page 41, *By the end of his time in Italy*: Quoted in Terry Comito, "Renaissance Gardens and the Discovery of Paradise," *Journal of the History of Ideas*, Vol. 32, No. 4 (Oct.–Dec. 1971), pp. 483–506. P. 483. Mawrey.

Page 41, *Even though it was January*: Jan L. De Jong, *The Power and the Glorification*. University Park, PA: Penn State UP, 2013, p. 38.

Page 42, *But as they settled in, the soldiers committed crimes*: Brenda J. Baker and George Armelagos, "The Origins and Antiquity of Syphilis," *Current Anthropology*, Vol. 29, No. 5, (Dec. 1988), p. 708.

Page 42, *Frightened and powerless, people blames their enemies*: M. Tampa et al, "A Brief History of Syphilis," *Journal of Medicine and Life*, (2014 Mar 15); 7(1), pp. 4–10. Available at https://www.ncbi.nlm.nih.gov/pmc/articles/PMC3956094/.

Page 43, *He'd begun writing the poem many years earlier*: Quoted in G. L. Hendrickson, "The 'Syphilis' of Girolamo Fracastoro: With Some Observations on the Origin and History of the Word 'Syphilis,'" *Bulletin of the Institute of the History of Medicine*, Vol. 2, No. 9 (November 1934), pp. 515–546, p. 519.

Page 45, *And last night, he proposed injecting disinfectants*: Quoted in Dartunnoro Clark, "Trump suggests 'injection' of disinfectant to beat coronavirus and 'clean' the lungs," NBC News, April 23, 2020. Available at https://www.nbcnews.com/politics/donald-trump/trump-suggests-injection-disinfectant-beat-coronavirus-clean-lungs-n1191216.

Page 46, *Part of what makes me so frustrated*: James C. Scott, *Against the Grain: A Deep History of the Earliest States*. New Haven: Yale University Press, 2017, p. 98.

Page 47, *People who are free, she wrote*: Quoted in Winham, p. 90.

Page 48, *Researchers believe that flu virus*: Mark Osborne Humphries, "Paths of Infection: The First World War and the Origins of the 1918 Influenza Pandemic," *War in History*, Vol. 21, No. 1 (January 2014), pp 55–81, p. 58.

Page 49, *In a letter to her brother*: Quoted in James E. Miller, Jr. *T. S. Eliot: The Making of an American Poet*. Penn State UP, 2005, p. 308.

Page 50, *A public health recommendation to avoid large crowds*: "Coronavirus: How they tried to curb Spanish flu pandemic in 1918," BBC News, 10 May 2020. Available at https://www.bbc.com/news/in-pictures-52564371.

Page 50, *In this news vacuum, conspiracy theories took hold*: Quoted in Robert Hume, "'Far too little, too late': what happened when Spanish Flu hit Britain?" *BBC History Magazine*, January 2018. (Available online at www.historyextra.com) https://www.historyextra.com/period/first-world-war/spanish-flu-britain-how-many-died-quarantine-

Page 51, *He quoted one survivor*: Quoted in Gabriel W. Kirkpatrick, "Influenza 1918: A Maine Perspective," Maine History, Vol. 25, No. 3, 1-1-1986, p. 175. Available at https://digitalcommons.library.umaine.edu/cgi/viewcontent.cgi?article=1523&context=mainehistoryjournal.

MAY

Page 58, *Early agriculturalists in the Andean highlands*: Jonathan D. Sauer, *Historical Geography of Crop Plants: A Select Roster*. Boca Raton, Fl: CRC Press, 1993. Kindle version (loc. 3533 of 8122).

Page 58, *The clay binds with the toxins*: Charles C. Mann, "How the Potato Changed the World," *Smithsonian Magazine*, November 2011. Available at https://www.smithsonianmag.com/history/how-the-potato-changed-the-world-108470605/.

Page 59, *Peruvian farmers continue to cultivate so many kinds*: In Mann, "How the Potato Changed the World."

Page 59, *Colors range from white to black*: John Reader, *Potato: A History of the Propitious Esculent*. New Haven: Yale University Press, 2008. Kindle edition (loc. 108).

Page 61, *Over time, as the ethnobotanist Gary Paul Nabhan noted*: Gary Paul Nabhan, *Cumin, Camels, and Caravans: A Spice Odyssey*. Berkeley: University of California Press, 2014, p. 21.

Page 62, *In India, Alexander's troops saw sugarcane*: A. J. Mangelsdorf, "Sugar-Cane: As Seen from Hawaii," *Economic Botany*, Vol. 4, No. 2 (Apr.–Jun. 1950), pp. 150–176, p. 150.

Page 62, *They were also amazed by shrubs*: Quoted in James Agustin Brown Scherer, *Cotton as a World Power: A Study in the Economic Interpretation of History, Vol. I*. New York: Frederick A. Stokes Co. 1916, p. 6.

Page 62, *As the Roman Empire expanded northward*: R. W. Davies, "The Roman Military Diet," *Britannia*, Vol. 2 (1971), pp. 133-134.

Page 66, *Even so, when a plague arrived*: Tom W. Hilliard, "Children and the Onset of the Athenian Plague," *Mediterranean Archaeology* (2006/2007), p. 157.

Page 66, All quotes in this section are from Book II, Chapter VII of The Internet Classics Archive: *The History of the Peloponnesian War* by Thucydides.

Page 68, *In "The Nature of Man," Hippocrates wrote*: Hippocrates, "The Nature of Man," in *Hippocratic Writings*. New York: Penguin, 1984, p. 255.

Page 68, *Likewise, Pliny the Elder thought onions*: Martha Jay, *Onions and Garlic: A Global History*. London: Reaktion Books, 2016, p. 27.

Page 68, *In fact, when Socrates described onions*: Xenophon, *The Symposium*, Chapter 4, Section 10.

JUNE

Page 74, *Last night, Stephen Colbert opened his monologue*: Steve Licht, Executive Producer, *The Colbert Show*, June 1, 2020.

Page 75, *Burroughs points to that as proof*: William S. Burroughs, *The Adding Machine: Selected Essays*. NY: Arcade Publishing, p. 47.

Page 77, *Science writer Ed Yong describes this embryonic development*: Ed Yong, *I Contain Multitudes: The Microbes Within Us and a Grander View of Life*. New York: Ecco (reprint, 2018), p. 53.

Page 78, *"There is no us and them"*: Carl Zimmer, *A Planet of Viruses*, 2nd edition. Chicago: University of Chicago Press, 2015, Kindle edition, loc. 731.

Page 78, *The scholar Donna Haraway has long insisted*: Donna Haraway, "Introduction: A Kinship of Feminist Figurations," *The Haraway Reader*. New York: Routledge, 2004, p. 2.

Page 80, *Henry David Thoreau pointed out that gardening involves killing*: Henry David Thoreau, *Walden, or Life in the Woods*, reprinted in the *Cambridge Edition of the Selected Works of Thoreau*, with a new introduction by Walter Harding. Boston: Houghton, Mifflin Co., 1975, p. 352.

Page 82, *In his book* Flight Ways, *Thom van Dooren offers a modification*: Thom van Dooren, *Flight Ways: Life and Loss at the Edge of Extinction*. New York: Columbia University Press, 2014, p. 60.

Page 90, *In her book of poems* This Connection of Everyone with Lungs: Juliana Spahr, "poem written after September 11/2001," in *This Connection of Everyone with Lungs: Poems*. Berkeley, CA: University of Berkeley Press, 2005, p. 6.

Page 91, *In fact, five of the six emperors*: Niccolo Machiavelli, *Discourses on Livy*, Translated by Harvey C. Mansfield and Nathan Tarcov. Chicago: University of Chicago Press, 1996, p. 32.

Page 92, *But the region became a viral hot spot*: Rebecca Flemming, "Galen and the Plague," In *Galen's Treatise Περὶ Ἀλυπίας () in Context: A Tale of Resilience*, edited by Caroline Petit, Brill, 2019, p. 223.

Page 92, *For people then, as for us*: Flemming, 241.

JULY

Page 96, *In a* New Yorker *essay last April*: Elizabeth Kolbert, "Pandemics and the Shape of Human History," *New Yorker,* April 6, 2020.

Page 98, *Procopius, a historian in that era*: Procopius, *Secret History.* Translated by Richard Atwater, reprinted Ann Arbor, MI: University of Michigan Press, 1961. Available at Fordham University Internet Medieval Sourcebook, https://sourcebooks.fordham.edu/basis/procop-anec.asp.

Page 99, *Justinian was a man* and subsequent notes in this paragraph: William Rosen, *Justinian's Flea: The First Great Plague and the End of the Roman Empire.* NY: Penguin Reprint, 2008, pp. 68–69, 73, 70.

Page 99, *Justinian's voracious egotism* and subsequent quotes in this paragraph: Rosen, pp. 73, 67, 77, 67, 69, 129.

Page 101, *It's extremely compact*: Daniel L. Everett, "Cultural Constraints on Grammar and Cognition in Pirahã: Another Look at the Design Features of Human Language," *Current Anthropology*, Vol. 46, No. 4 (Aug–Oct 2005). Available at https://www1.icsi.berkeley.edu/~kay/Everett.CA.Piraha.pdf. For comparison, English has forty-four speech sounds.

Page 111, *And in the third generation*: Gregor Mendel, "Experiments in Plant Hybridization (1865)" Read at the February 8 and March 8, 1865, meetings of the Brünn Natural History Society, p. 13. Available at http://www.esp.org/foundations/genetics/classical/gm-65.pdf.

Page 113, *Others theorized the seeds were American in origin*: Chris Heath, "The Truth Behind the Amazon Mystery Seeds," *The Atlantic*, July 15, 2021. Available at https://www.theatlantic.com/science/archive/2021/07/unsolicited-seeds-china-brushing/619417/.

AUGUST

Page 120, *Some Florentines decided "living moderately"* and subsequent quote: Giovanni Boccaccio, *The Decameron*, Norton Critical Edition translated and edited by Wayne Rebhorn. New York: W. W. Norton & Co., 2016. P. 7.

Page 120, *Still others pursued a middle way, "neither restricting"* and subsequent quotes in this paragraph: Boccaccio, p. 8.

Page 121, *A plague treatise from 1348 recommended*: Christiane Nockels Fabbri, "Treating Medieval Plague: The Wonderful Virtues of Theriac," *Early Science and Medicine*, Vol. 12, No. 3 (2007), p. 263.

Page 122, *Reflecting on the plague, which killed both his parents*: Ibn Khaldûn, *The Muqaddimah: An Introduction to History,* Translated and Introduced by Franz Rosenthal, Abridged and Edited by N.J. Dawood. Princeton: Princeton University Press, 1967, p. 83.

Page 129, *Blake calls this process "biosocial entanglement"*: Michael Blake, *Maize for the Gods: Unearthing the 9,000-Year History of Corn*. California: University of California Press, 2015, p. 22.

Page 130, *Fermented, it's chicha*: Blake, p. 202.

Page 131, *From them, he "started to do a fairly significant giveaway"*: Quoted in Meredith Goad, "Albie Barden preserves native varieties of flint corn for future generations." *Portland Press Herald*, October 2, 2016. Available online at https://www.pressherald.com/2016/10/02/corn-keeper-albie-barden-is-preserving-native-varieties-of-flint-corn-for-future-generations/.

Page 135, *And "invasive" plants are non-native*: Presidential Executive Order 13112 (February 1999).

Page 143, *And in* Rolling Stone *this month* and subsequent quotes in this paragraph: Wade Davis, "The Unraveling of America," *Rolling Stone*, August 6, 2020. Available at https://www.rollingstone.com/politics/political-commentary/covid-19-end-of-american-era-wade-davis-1038206/.

SEPTEMBER

Page 146, *When Henry David Thoreau wrote*: Thoreau, p. 346.

Page 149, *He brought "stones and seeds of European orchard trees"*: Stephen A. Spongberg, "Notes on Transatlantic Migrants," *Arnoldia*, Vol. 53, No. 2 (1993), p. 11.

Page 152, *In January 1836, Charles Darwin wrote*: Charles Darwin, *Journal*, Chapter XIX, January 12, 1836.

Page 153, *For centuries, inhabitants of the islands*: Alfred W. Crosby, Jr., "The Early History of Syphilis: A Reappraisal," *American Anthropologist*, Vol. 71, No. 2 (Apr. 1969, 218–227), p. 222.

Page 154, *Rather,* T. pallidum *was the cause of the syphilis pandemic*: Brenda W. Baker, George J. Armelagos and others. "The Origin and Antiquity of Syphilis: Paleopathological Diagnosis and Interpretation [and Comments and Reply]," *Current Anthropology*, Vol. 29, No. 5 (Dec. 1988), p. 719. Not everyone agrees that this is the origin of syphilis; two other possibilities are also put forth, but this is the prevailing theory.

Page 154, *Then, "pustules often covered the body"*: Jared Diamond, "The Arrow of Disease," *Discovery*, January 18, 1992. Available at https://www.discovermagazine.com/health/the-arrow-of-disease.

Page 154, *A writer in 1519 described "boils that stood out like Acorns"*: Quoted in Lizzie Buchen, "First Rule of Being a Successful STD," *Discover*, April 29, 2008. Available at https://www.discovermagazine.com/planet-earth/first-rule-of-being-a-successful-std-make-sure-the-host-still-has-sex.

Page 154, *More than 150 years after the first syphilis epidemic*: John Wynell, *Lues venera wherein the names, nature, subject, causes, signes, and cure, are handled, mistakes in these discovered, rectified, doubts and questions succinctly resolved.* London, 1660. Available online at https://quod.lib.umich.edu/e/eebo2/A67222.0001.001/.

Page 155, *Instead, I am trying to hold on to*: Thoreau, p. 359.

Page 158, *According to the catalogue copy*: Catalog available online at https://www.victoryseeds.com/tomato_brandywine-yellow.html.

Page 162, *David Landreth, the seedsman*: Saint Louis Mercantile Association, *Seed for thought: an exhibition of early seed catalogues, horticultural manuals and illustrated books related to 19th and 20th century American gardening*. Saint Louis, MO: Tomkins Printing Company, 1988, entry 19.

Page 163, *They wanted fruits of uniform size*: Clarissa Hyman, *Tomato: A Global History*. London: Reaktion Books Ltd., 2019, p.79.

Page 164, *Yesterday, an article about language trends*: "How COVID-19 is changing the English Language," *The Conversation.com*. Published September 25, 2020, 8:26 am. Available at https://theconversation.com/how-covid-19-is-changing-the-english-language-146171.

Page 166, *In a* New York Times *article marking it* and subsequent quote in this paragraph: Richard Pérez-Peña, "Coronavirus Deaths Pass One Million Worldwide," *The New York Times*, September 28, 2020, Available online at https://www.nytimes.com/2020/09/28/world/covid-1-million-deaths.html.

OCTOBER

Page 170, *Quammen points out that*: David Quammen, "We Made the Coronavirus Epidemic," *The New York Times,* Jan. 28, 2020.

Page 175, *In 1539, a friar who accompanied Pizarro's party*: Quoted in Rebecca Earle, *Feeding the People: The Politics of the Potato*. Cambridge: Cambridge University Press, 2020, p. 23.

Page 175, *Herbalists in the sixteenth and seventeenth centuries*: Earle, 31.

Page 175, *"If the Irish had united"*: Henry Hobhouse, *Seeds of Change: Six Plants that Transformed Mankind*. Berkeley, CA: Counterpoint, 2005, p. 247.

Page 176, *The crop historian Jonathan Sauer wrote*: Sauer, kindle edition (loc. 3632 of 8122).

Page 182, *Chile "seeds tether us to the land"*: Isaura Andaluz, "Celebrating the Chile Nativo." In *Seed Sovereignty, Food Security: Women in the Vanguard of the Fight Against GMOs and Corporate Agriculture,* edited by Vandana Shiva, 237–48. Berkeley, CA: North Atlantic Books, p. 237.

Page 186, *John McQuaid explains that at "around 300 degrees Fahrenheit"*: John McQuaid, *Tasty: The Art and Science of What We Eat*. New York: Scribner reprint edition, 2015, p. 39.

NOVEMBER

Page 194, *He wrote to a friend*: Quoted in Andrea Wulf, *Founding Gardeners: The Revolutionary Generation, Nature, and the Shaping of the American Nation*. New York: Knopf, 1994, p 143.

Page 195, *Benjamin Franklin sent home*: Nelson Klose, *America's Crop Heritage: The History of Foreign Plant Introduction by the Federal Government*. Ames, IA: Iowa State College Press, 1950, p. 14.

Page 195, *Though George Washington didn't introduce any novel plants*: Quoted in Kathy J. Cooke, "'Who Wants White Carrots?': Congressional Seed Distribution, 1862 to 1923," *The Journal of the Gilded Age and Progressive Era* 17 (2018), 475–500, p. 475.

Page 196, *For these statesmen, as Andrea Wulf observed*: Wulf, 10.

Page 196, *But afterward, John Adams feared*: Quoted in Wulf, 115.

Page 197, *In 1794, in a letter, Washington wrote*: Washington quote is in Wulf, 116; Jefferson quotes are in Edmund Fulling, "Thomas Jefferson: His Interest in Plant Life as Revealed in his Writings-I," *Bulletin of the Torrey Botanical Club*, Vol. 71, No. 6 (Nov. 1944), p. 585.

Page 197, *Andrea Wulf wrote*: Wulf, *Founding Gardeners*, p. 10.

Page 200, *Indeed, Michael Pollan notes*: Michael Pollan, *The Botany of Desire: A Plant's-Eye View of the World*. New York: Random House, 2001, p. 12.

Page 201, *The seeds for those trees had been gathered*: Pollan, pp. 11, 55.

DECEMBER

Page 214, *According to Plutarch*: John Stolarczyk and Jules Janick, "Carrot: History and Iconography," *Chronica Horticulturae*, Vol. 51, No. 2 (2011), pp. 13–18. p. 14.

Page 215, *Instead, people described what we think of as orange*: "Carrot History: AD 200 to 1500," World Carrot Museum. Internet archive available at http://www.carrotmuseum.co.uk/history3.html.

Page 216, *He complained that a "great aboundance of carrets"* and subsequent quotes in this paragraph: Richard Gardiner, *Profitable instructions for the Manuring, Sowing and Planting of Kitchin Gardens*. London: Edward Allde, 1599. Available online at https://famineanddearth.exeter.ac.uk/displayhtml.html?id=fp_00143_en_profitableinsructionsfor.

Page 217, *When Michelle Obama established a White House Garden*: Arlette Saenz, "Michelle Obama's White House Kitchen Garden Includes a Vegetable You've Probably Never Heard Of," ABC News, June 3, 2015, 8:08 pm. Available at https://abcnews.go.com/Politics/michelle-obamas-white house-kitchen-garden-includes-vegetable/story?id=31509613.

Page 218, *"In an infant country"*: Quoted in Klose, p. 17.

Page 218, *In 1819, the secretary of the treasury asked naval officers*: Quoted in Klose, p. 26.

Page 218, *Similarly, during his presidency*: Quote in Klose, 27.

Page 220, *A few hours after the electoral college finished*: Quoted in Elise Viebeck et al., "Electoral college affirms Biden's victory on a relatively calm day of a chaotic election." *The Washington Post*, December 14, 2020.

Page 223, *The immunity—or lack thereof—of those around us*: Eula Biss, *On Immunity: An Inoculation*, Minneapolis, MN: Graywolf Press, 2014. Kindle version, loc. 230 of 2624.

Three lines from "Winter Song for One Who Suffers" from *In a Few Minutes Before Later* © 2022 by Brenda Hillman. Published by Wesleyan University Press. Used with permission.

ACKNOWLEDGMENTS

For a book that chronicles a year spent in relative isolation, it—and I—have quite a few people to thank for their kindnesses and help. First, last, and always, huge gratitude to my husband, Rob, who braved the bigger world when doing so was terrifying and who encouraged me to write into—and through—the awful uncertainty. Big thanks to several folks who aided me in seed-sleuthing journeys before the pandemic that are mentioned here. Thank you to Neil Lash and Isaura Andaluz, for sharing your wisdom and giving me tours of the seed banks you steward. And thank you to the staff of the Plant Genetic Resources Unit in Geneva, New York, who trusted me to wander through their orchards for two glorious afternoons. Deep thanks to Juliana Spahr for her poetry and for allowing me to quote from it in this book. A shout out to the staff of Maine Farmland Trust's Joseph Fiore Art Center: when their artist-in-residence program could not take place in person in 2020, they pivoted (that word!) and created a virtual version. Thank you to Katie, James, and Sophie, my cohort for that virtual residency, for your camaraderie and early feedback on the essay that morphed into this book. To the members of the St. George COVID-19 Task Force—Kate, Beckie, Wayne, Linda, Mike, Alane, Rob, John, Jake, and Amy: you helped me retain my faith in community and the importance of leaning into interconnectedness through that long, strange year. And to Laura, Tom, Susan, Mark, and Kate: thank you, of course, for your friendship—and also for gamely embracing the bittersweet pleasure of the outdoor, socially distanced, potluck cocktail hour. Finally, a huge thank you to the intrepid team at Godine, especially Joshua Bodwell, Celia Johnson, Beth Blachman, and David Allender; you are a blessing.

A NOTE ABOUT THE AUTHOR

Margot Anne Kelley is a writer and photographer whose work focuses on the natural world. Her previous book with Godine, *Foodtopia*, was a winner of a *Readable Feast* Book Award, a finalist for the Maine Literary Award in Nonfiction, and a *Civil Eats'* Food and Farming Book Pick. Kelley has served as the editor of *The Maine Review* and co-founded a community development corporation which runs a food pantry and community garden, among other programs. She lives in Port Clyde, Maine.

A NOTE ON THE TYPE

A Gardener at the End of the World has been set in Garamond. While our modern version was designed by Robert Slimbach, it is based on the typefaces created by famed French printer Claude Garamond, a driving force behind typeface design during the Renaissance period in the sixteenth century. The oblique nature of the slimmest areas found in the Garamond's shapes make the typeface exceedingly graceful in print.

Design & Composition by Tammy Ackerman

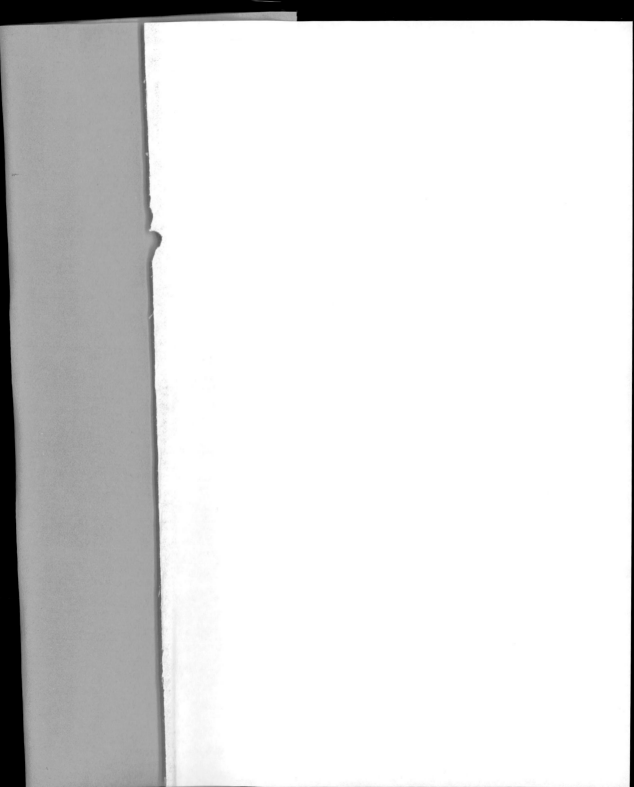